Robert Downey Jr.

Superhero Superstar

By Nicole Horning

Portions of this book originally appeared in
Robert Downey Jr. by Laurie Collier Hillstrom.

Published in 2020 by
Lucent Press, an Imprint of Greenhaven Publishing, LLC
353 3rd Avenue
Suite 255
New York, NY 10010

Designer: Deanna Paternostro
Editor: Nicole Horning

Cataloging-in-Publication Data

Names: Horning, Nicole.
Title: Robert Downey Jr.: superhero superstar / Nicole Horning.
Description: New York : Lucent Press, 2020. | Series: People in the news |
Includes index.
Identifiers: ISBN 9781534567696 (pbk.) | ISBN 9781534567054 (library bound) |
ISBN 9781534567702 (ebook)
Subjects: LCSH: Downey, Robert, 1965- Juvenile literature. | Actors–United States-
-Biography–Juvenile literature.
Classification: LCC PN2287.D548 H56 2020 | DDC 791.4302'8092 B–dc23

Printed in the United States of America

CPSIA compliance information: Batch #BS19KL: For further information contact Greenhaven Publishing LLC, New York,
New York, at 1-844-317-7404.

Please visit our website, www.greenhavenpublishing.com. For a free color
catalog of all our high-quality books, call toll free 1-844-317-7404 or fax
1-844-317-7405.

Contents

Foreword

We live in a world where the latest news is always available and where it seems we have unlimited access to the lives of the people in the news. Entire television networks are devoted to news about politics, sports, and entertainment. Social media has allowed people to have an unprecedented level of interaction with celebrities. We have more information at our fingertips than ever before. However, how much do we really know about the people we see on television news programs, social media feeds, and magazine covers?

Despite the constant stream of news, the full stories behind the lives of some of the world's most newsworthy men and women are often unknown. Who was Gal Gadot before she became Wonder Woman? What does LeBron James do when he is not playing basketball? What inspires Lin-Manuel Miranda?

This series aims to answer questions like these about some of the biggest names in pop culture, sports, politics, and technology. While the subjects of this series come from all walks of life and areas of expertise, they share a common magnetism that has made them all captivating figures in the public eye. They have shaped the world in some unique way, and—in many cases—they are poised to continue to shape the world for many years to come.

These biographies are not just a collection of basic facts. They tell compelling stories that show how each figure grew to become a powerful public personality. Each book aims to paint a complete, realistic picture of its subject—from the challenges they overcame to the controversies they caused. In doing so, each book reinforces the idea that even the most famous faces on the news are real people who are much more complex than we are often shown in brief video clips or sound bites. Readers are also reminded that there is even more to a person than what they present to the world through social media posts, press releases, and interviews. The whole story of a person's life can only be discovered by digging beneath the surface of their public persona, and that is what this series allows readers to do.

The books in this series are filled with enlightening quotes from speeches and interviews given by the subjects, as well as quotes and anecdotes from those who know their story best: family, friends, coaches, and colleagues. All quotes are noted to provide guidance for further research. Detailed lists of additional resources are also included, as are timelines, indexes, and unique photographs. These text features come together to enhance the reading experience and encourage readers to dive deeper into the stories of these influential men and women.

Fame can be fleeting, but the subjects featured in this series have real staying power. They have fundamentally impacted their respective fields and have achieved great success through hard work and true talent. They are men and women defined by their accomplishments, and they are often seen as role models for the next generation. They have left their mark on the world in a major way, and their stories are meant to inspire readers to leave their mark, too.

Robert Downey Jr.: Box Office Superstar

Robert Downey Jr. is one of the most popular actors in Hollywood. He started acting in small roles as a child in his father's movies in the 1970s and went on to be a critically acclaimed actor in the 1990s. However, the role that has catapulted Downey into box office superstardom is that of Tony Stark/Iron Man in the Marvel Cinematic Universe (MCU). Downey was in the process of recovering from personal issues in his life when Marvel started planning a line of movies centered on the core members of the Avengers and, eventually, a series of *Avengers* movies as well. The first movie released in the MCU was *Iron Man*, with Downey in the title role. However, while most casual viewers and devoted fans would say that he was perfect for the role, getting there took a lot of hard work from Downey to overcome hesitation on behalf of the production company because of Downey's past.

A Celebrated and Respected Actor

Downey has been in more than 60 films throughout his career and acted in TV shows such as *Ally McBeal*. While the sheer amount of movies Downey has starred in is impressive on its own, his versatility and what he brings to each role he takes on is what makes him one of the most celebrated and respected actors in Hollywood. Downey has starred in a variety of comedies, dramas, and thrillers that have earned him more than 100 award nominations and more than 30 awards won. As reviewer Jim Emerson wrote, "He consistently brings more to his material than the part demands. Whether the movie itself doesn't measure up to him ('Less Than Zero,' 'Chaplin'), or is very good indeed ('Short Cuts,' 'Wonder Boys,' 'Zodiac'), he contributes something that makes it—or, at least, him—something to see."[1]

Throughout the 1980s, Downey was in a handful of movies that reviewers stated were largely forgettable, and it was said that Downey was the "best thing in a lot of bad movies."[2] In the 1990s, however, that started to change with his role in the film *Chaplin*. In 1992, Downey portrayed the legendary silent film star Charlie Chaplin. While the movie itself was called disappointing by some critics, Downey's performance as the silent film star received rave reviews. As the late film reviewer Roger Ebert wrote, "Robert Downey Jr. succeeds almost uncannily in playing Chaplin; the physical resemblance is convincing, but better is the way Downey captures Chaplin's spirit, even in costume."[3] In 1993, at not even 30 years old, Downey was nominated for an Academy Award for Best Actor in a Leading Role for his work as Chaplin. The positive reviews for Downey were even more remarkable because few people believed he could play the role. *Chaplin*'s director, Sir Richard Attenborough, was one of the few people who had faith in Downey and his work—Downey beat out 30 other actors for the role. Attenborough considered actors such as Robin Williams, Dustin Hoffman, and Billy Crystal for the role and screen-tested seven actors, one of which was Downey. Downey was awarded the role based on his physical similarities to Chaplin, ability to mimic, and screen test. Even though the movie as a whole was not universally beloved by critics, Downey's casting was spot on.

Robert Downey Jr. was praised for his similarities to Charlie Chaplin (left) in the movie *Chaplin*. These similarities are also what earned him the role after his screen test.

From Outcast to Iron Man

Despite this success, in the mid-1990s, Downey's career started to be marred by tabloid headlines and problems with alcohol and drug addiction. In 1996, he was pulled over by police and found in possession of heroin and cocaine, and throughout the rest of the 1990s and into the early 2000s, Downey was afflicted with a drug addiction, was arrested a number of times, and spent time in prison. As a result, "for a period in the 1990s and the early part of the next decade, the actor was considered a pariah [outcast] and a laughing stock, despite (or perhaps because of) the fact that he had consistently hailed himself as the best actor of his generation after the intensity of his performances, not least in his Oscar-nominated role in the biopic *Chaplin* in 1992."[4] However, in the early 2000s, Downey began to recover from his drug addiction and began to rebuild his career, which started with his role in *The Singing Detective* in 2003. Following this, Downey met his future wife, who helped him turn his life around for good and demanded that he give up drugs permanently.

This hard part of Downey's life meant that when the time came for casting the role of Tony Stark/Iron Man in *Iron Man*, there was a lot of hesitation on behalf of the production company. However, after his screen test, the conclusion was reached that there was no one else who could play the role, and Marvel fans generally agree with this. What Downey brings to this character is even greater considering the trials he has gone through throughout his own life.

Following the first *Iron Man* movie, Downey's career skyrocketed, resulting in roles in *Tropic Thunder* and *Sherlock Holmes*. Additionally, since the first *Iron Man* movie, the MCU has greatly expanded with massively successful movies, with Downey playing one of the principal characters. Downey has starred in two *Iron Man* sequels, four *Avengers* movies, *Captain America: Civil War*, and *Spider-Man: Homecoming*. The hard road he took for a while gave greater depth to the characters he portrayed, such as Tony Stark, and the experience of traveling such a hard road helped him truly appreciate his newfound peace and contentment that has come from being sober and having a family. Downey said, "I used to be so convinced that happiness was the goal, yet all those years I was chasing after it, I was unhappy in the pursuit," he explained. "Maybe the goal should really be a life that values honour, duty, good work, friends and family ... maybe happiness follows from that."[5] While Downey's portrayal of Tony Stark/Iron Man is thrilling for fans to watch, especially because Downey and the character he plays often seem to be essentially one and the same, the road he took to get there

Robert Downey Jr. is shown here assembled with most of the Avengers at the *Avengers: Infinity War* premiere in April 2018.

was filled with personal issues and a lot of hard work. It led, however, to him becoming one of the most respected actors in the film industry.

Chapter One

Destined
for Films

On April 4, 1965, Robert Downey Jr. was born in New York City to Robert Downey Sr. and Elsie Ford Downey. Robert and his older sister, Allyson, were raised in Greenwich Village, a neighborhood in Manhattan. Robert was destined to be involved in the movie business, given that he grew up in a creative atmosphere—his father was an independent film-maker, and his mother was an actress. Additionally, at the young age of five, Robert played a puppy in his father's 1970 movie *Pound*, and he would end up having small parts in his father's films from that point on. This creative atmosphere and the partying life that went along with it impacted the rest of Robert's life.

The Beginning of an Acting Career

Robert Downey Jr. made his first appearance as an actor in one of his dad's movies when he was five years old. "He did it because it was better than having a babysitter," his father explained. "But it might have led him to believe that to be creative was much better than trying to get a regular job."[6]

This first acting role was in *Pound*, a wacky social satire set in a New York City animal shelter. The movie featured

Filmmaker and Father: Robert Downey Sr.

Robert Downey Sr.'s name at birth was Robert Elias, after his biological father. His mother was a model whose image appeared on the cover of several popular magazines. After his parents split up, his mother married James Downey and moved with her son to New York City.

At the age of 16, Robert left home in search of adventure. He enlisted in the U.S. Army using his stepfather's last name and a fake birth certificate, and he went by Robert Downey from that time onward. After receiving a dishonorable discharge from the service for fighting, Downey won a Golden Gloves boxing title and played semiprofessional baseball for a few years.

In 1960, Downey returned to New York City, where he made a living by waiting tables, acting, writing plays and screenplays, and working for an alternative film editor. The following year, he launched his career as an independent filmmaker, which eventually encompassed nearly 20 films. Some of his early works are considered groundbreaking achievements in the underground, experimental film movement.

18 human actors, each of whom portrayed a different breed of dog or cat that was waiting to be adopted. The actors dressed up in clothing that represented their breed in a humorous way. A man in a silk robe played a boxer, for example, while a man in a jogging suit played a greyhound. Robert played a puppy with an attitude.

Two years later, at the age of seven, Robert appeared in his

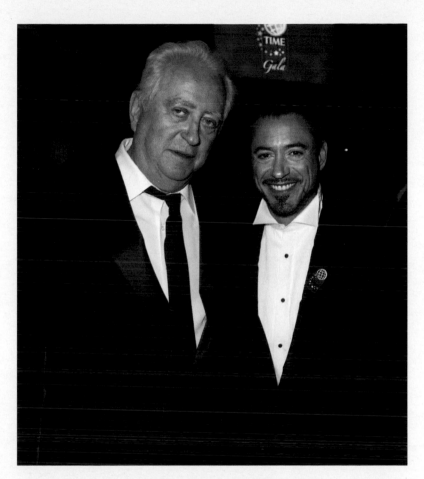

Robert Downey Jr. is shown here with his father at a *TIME* magazine gala.

father's first big-budget movie, *Greaser's Palace*. Shot in the desert outside of Santa Fe, New Mexico, it was a surrealistic Western that loosely followed stories from the Bible and included scenes that could have been frightening for such a young child, especially when the child was acting in that specific scene. "It could have been too much to expose him to," Downey Sr. acknowledged. "It was traumatic for him to see that kind of violence. He didn't comprehend that everybody comes back again"[7] when the scene is over.

Despite the fact that his father's movies could be strange and sometimes frightening, Robert never questioned the idea of acting in them. Still, he understood that his family life was very unusual compared with that of his friends and classmates. "I didn't want to talk about what my dad did because it wasn't like he was directing *All in the Family* [a hit TV show of the 1970s] or anything," he said. "He was doing these crazy films. Mom would pick me up at school wearing this big quilted cape. I felt like I was in a J. D. Salinger [author of the famous novel *The Catcher in the Rye*] story."[8]

Robert Downey Jr. grew up in a creative atmosphere and started acting at a young age in his father's movies.

An Unusual Childhood

Another way in which Robert's childhood was unusual was the presence of drugs and alcohol in his home. His parents and their friends frequently smoked marijuana and occasionally used other drugs, and they did not hide this drug use from the children. Hippies and artists in the liberal atmosphere of the 1960s   when millions of Americans rebelled against the social constraints and conservative ideas of the past—viewed the use of mind-altering substances as acceptable. However, given the amount of knowledge on these substances that people have today, this behavior is seen as dangerous and unacceptable, especially in front of children.

Growing up in this environment, Robert was exposed to drugs at an early age. Beginning between six and eight years old, his father allowed him to smoke marijuana. Although Downey Sr. did not give much thought to the decision at the time, he eventually realized how irresponsible and dangerous it had been to allow Robert to try drugs. "We thought it was cute to let them smoke it and all," he recalled. "It was an idiot move on our parts."[9] Robert refused to blame his father for his later drug addiction, however. He claimed that his father's casual attitude toward drugs—and willingness to share them with him—reflected the permissive nature of the times.

As Robert approached his teen years, his unusual home environment took a greater toll on him emotionally and socially. Since his parents often shot their films on location, the family moved around a lot. Robert spent parts of his childhood in upstate New York, Connecticut, California, and London, England. He went to a number of different schools, and his grades and attendance records reflected these struggles. One result of the frequent moves and personal struggles was the fight for attention. For example, "He once jumped into our friend's Volvo, and even though he didn't know how to drive, he backed up into a car and went forward over a curb,"[10] remembered school friend Anthony D'Eugenio.

As Robert grew older, his father sank deeper into drug use, which reduced his film output and put the family into debt.

Acting Classes

Robert Downey Jr. did not take acting classes or go to drama school before finding success as an actor. He is not the only actor to find success without formal dramatic training. While drama school can help a young actor develop their talents and meet people who can help them in their career, it is not necessary for this career path. Some famous actors have gotten their start with roles in television shows and films without going to acting school—Michael B. Jordan, who played Erik Killmonger in the MCU film *Black Panther*, got his start in this way and went on to become an incredibly successful actor.

Other actors, such as Chris Pratt, have been discovered in unconventional places. Pratt, who plays Peter Quill/Star-Lord in the MCU's *Guardians of the Galaxy* series, was living out of his car and waiting tables at a restaurant when he was discovered by a director.

However, drama programs can be helpful—some recent programs have taught classes on podcasting, while others have had students act with an artificial intelligence machine. As Nick Asbury wrote in the *Guardian*, "There are two main reasons to go to drama school: the first is to learn something ... The second reason is to meet people who are going to give you jobs. Agents use the main drama schools as a filter system. They can take actors on, fresh from school, and then put them in front of casting directors."[1] For example, Chris Evans (Steve Rogers/Captain America in the MCU) and

His parents divorced in 1978, and Downey Sr. moved to Los Angeles, California, to take a job in the film industry. Allyson decided to move to Los Angeles with him, and Robert agreed

Acting classes are not always needed to begin an acting career. Chris Pratt (left) was discovered at a restaurant, and Tom Hiddleston (right) extensively studied acting. Both actors went on to have incredibly successful careers.

Scarlett Johansson (Natasha Romanoff/Black Widow in the MCU) both attended acting programs at the Lee Strasberg Theater and Film Institute in New York, while Tom Hiddleston (Loki in the MCU) went to the Royal Academy of Dramatic Art in London, England.

1. Nick Asbury, "Drama School a Waste of Time? Not Necessarily—But It Costs Too Much," *Guardian*, October 25, 2013. www.theguardian.com/stage/2013/oct/25/drama-school-waste-money-time-paul-roseby.

to stay with his mom in New York. Money was tight, however, and they could afford only a tiny, fifth-story walk-up apartment with bars on the windows. Feeling shaken and depressed from his family splitting, Robert began experimenting with harder drugs. "I was not dealing with my life in an effective manner," he admitted. "Instead, I was creating a separate reality from the one in which I now lived and was dealing with that reality the best I could."[11]

Santa Monica High School

While Robert and his mother struggled in New York, his father found some high-paying jobs in the film industry. Every time Robert went out to visit his father, he enjoyed the sunny, comfortable, laid-back vibe of Southern California. Additionally, the small apartment he lived in with his mom was not comfortable for either of them. Therefore, when he was 14, he decided to move across the country. "I came out to California and lived with Dad," he said. "I wanted to have, you know, a teen-age scene. You go from the one-room apartment on 48th Street to the house with the pool"[12] in Santa Monica.

After completing the eighth grade at Lincoln Junior High School in Santa Monica, Downey enrolled at Santa Monica High School. Known locally as Samohi, the school was located a few blocks from the beach. Among the student body were the sons and daughters of many big-name Hollywood talents. Robert became close friends with Ramón Estevez, the son of actor Martin Sheen and the brother of actors Charlie Sheen and Emilio Estevez.

Going to school with the children of famous TV and movie stars—many of whom had received formal acting, singing, and dancing lessons—made Robert feel a bit insecure about his small parts in his dad's independent films. "I didn't get trained in drama school. It was all on the job," he noted. "That [stuff] costs money; my dad was an underground filmmaker. I was faking it, to try to fit in."[13] What he lacked in formal training, however, he made up for in attitude. Additionally, he became a member of the school's elite chorus, which won a number of singing competitions, and won a leading role in Santa Monica High's production of the musical *Oklahoma!*

However, even after moving to California, Downey often skipped school to drink alcohol with his friends. As a consequence of his substance abuse, he got arrested for driving under the influence before he even got his driver's license. He recalled that one night he wanted to drive his friend's mom's car: "I got my hands on the keys, I went driving, I got lost, I pulled over to ask a police officer directions before he pulled me over to ask if I had a license—and I was shortly thereafter in custody."[14]

Pursuing Acting Full Time

In 1982, after two years at Santa Monica High School, Robert's father gave him the option to "either show up [to school] every day or quit and get a job."[15] At the young age of around 16, Downey chose to drop out and move to New York to pursue acting. Shortly after arriving in New York, he was cast in the play *American Passion*. Downey took the role seriously and was dedicated and focused on his part in it. This dedication paid off because it did not take him long to get an agent. As Downey said, "If I didn't get there an hour and a half before curtain, I wasn't going to be ready." He added, "The other people would roll in at a half-hour, and I'd be stretching out or doing some fake yoga, and they'd say, 'Robert's going to Nirvana before the show.' But I was the only one who got an agent two weeks later."[16] Downey finally began the career he had been destined for.

Chapter Two

A Rising Star

Once he had an agent, Downey steadily picked up roles. To start with, these roles were small, and in the film *Baby It's You*, most of Downey's scenes ended up being cut. However, he still gained valuable experience, and from this point, he went on to have roles in movies such as *Firstborn* and *Weird Science*, both of which were significant in regards to Downey's personal life as well. *Firstborn*, a 1984 film directed by Michael Apted, was a drama about two boys trying to make their divorced mother see that her new boyfriend is not what he seems. The film did not advance Downey's career much, but on the set of the movie, he met actress Sarah Jessica Parker, whom he would date for the next seven years.

The 1985 film *Weird Science* was a more significant role for Downey. *Weird Science* was one of a string of popular 1980s teen movies directed by John Hughes, who also worked on 1984's *Sixteen Candles* and 1985's *The Breakfast Club*. *Weird Science*'s plot involved two teenage boys, played by Anthony Michael Hall and Ilan Mitchell-Smith, who use technology to create their idea of a perfect woman. Downey played Ian, a bully who torments the boys. While his character torments Hall's and Mitchell-Smith's characters in the movie, off the set of the movie, Hall and Downey became close friends. This

Robert Downey Jr. and Sarah Jessica Parker met on the set of the movie *Firstborn* and started a relationship that lasted seven years.

friendship with Hall also ended up giving Downey's career the spark it needed.

Rising to Prominence

Downey's relationship with Hall paid off in the fall of 1985. TV producer Lorne Michaels—creator of the famous late-night sketch-comedy series *Saturday Night Live* (*SNL*)—was looking for a group of young, relatively unknown actors for the show. Ratings for *SNL* had been dropping since 1980, when Michaels left and took much of the writing crew and cast with him. When he returned to the show in 1985, he had to build it up again to the popular series it was before, and therefore, he was looking for new young talent to fill out the cast. Hall had come to his attention through his roles in *Sixteen Candles*, *The Breakfast Club*, and other teen classics of the 1980s. When Michaels invited Hall to join the cast of *SNL*, Hall suggested that the producer also give Downey an audition. Downey took advantage of the opportunity and earned a spot on the show. Throughout the 1985 to 1986 season of *SNL*, he amused audiences with his dead-on impersonations of famous people such as singer George Michael of Wham! and actor and director Sean Penn.

While he was shooting *SNL* in New York, Downey also made frequent trips across the country to appear in movies. He played a fairly prominent role in 1986's *Back to School*, a comedy starring Rodney Dangerfield as a jovial, self-made millionaire who decides to accompany his son to college. Downey played the son's rebellious roommate, Derek. Director Alan Metter appreciated Downey's ability to improvise and play off other actors in order to increase the comic value of certain scenes. In one scene, for example, Downey's character rushes into a room to deliver a message to Dangerfield's character. Finding a couch blocking his entrance, the actor simply vaulted over it and delivered his lines.

The charm, humor, and versatility Downey showed on

The Pick-Up Artist did not receive good reviews from critics, but it helped advance Downey's career because he played one of the lead roles. Downey is shown here with Molly Ringwald, who played Randy Jensen, the other lead role in the film.

SNL and in his film work brought him to the attention of screenwriter and director James Toback. Toback was looking for an actor with these qualities to play a leading role in his film *The Pick-Up Artist*, released in 1987. He gave Downey the role of Jack Jericho, who, as the movie title says, is a pick-up artist who tries to meet and start relationships with women. Downey starred opposite actress Molly Ringwald, who is known for her roles in *The Breakfast Club* and *Pretty in Pink*. Downey was excited to graduate to leading-man status after playing so many supporting roles. Although *The Pick-Up Artist* received generally unfavorable reviews, it did elevate him to a new level of prominence.

A Turning Point

As Downey's acting career began to take off, however, his drug and alcohol use increased as well. His steadily expanding film roles gave him the resources to maintain homes in both New York and Los Angeles—both of which he shared with Parker. He was also part of a crowd of popular young actors that included Billy Zane (known for his roles as Match in *Back to the Future* and Cal in *Titanic*) and Kiefer Sutherland (known for his roles as David in *The Lost Boys* and Jack Bauer in *24*). Downey and his friends drank, smoked marijuana, and soon progressed to using cocaine. Although Parker was concerned about her boyfriend's escalating substance abuse, she tried to limit its impact on his career. "I believed I was the person holding him together," she explained. "In every good and bad way I enabled him to get up in the morning and show up for work. If he did not, I was there to cover for him, find him, clean him up, and get him to the set or theatre."[17]

For his next project, Downey created a compelling portrait of a drug addict in the 1987 film *Less Than Zero*. Based on a best-selling novel by Bret Easton Ellis, the movie focuses on a group of young, attractive, and extremely wealthy—but also bored, self-absorbed, and cynical—friends hanging out and partying in Los Angeles. Downey played Julian Wells, a charismatic cocaine addict who spirals downward into debt and eventually self-destructs. Although the movie received mixed reviews, critics raved about Downey's haunting performance as Julian. "In many ways, *Less Than Zero* is a cynical, manipulative job," David Denby wrote in *New York* magazine. "Yet, the movie has something great in it, something that could legitimately move teenagers (or anyone else): Robert Downey Jr. as the disintegrating Julian, a performance in which beautiful exuberance gives way horrifyingly to a sudden, startled sadness."[18]

However, after seeing Downey's performance in the film, his friends worried about the extent to which the decline of Julian paralleled the actor's deepening drug addiction in real life. "*Less Than Zero* was a low point in his life," said Jami Gertz, who played Julian's girlfriend who tries unsuccessfully to save him. "The scenes were so true to life. It was all happening to him. You had the feeling, is this guy going to make it? Is what happens to Julian going to happen to Robert?"[19] Looking back on the experience, Downey agrees that it marked a turning point in his struggle with drug addiction. "Until that movie, I took my drugs after work and on the weekends. Maybe I'd turn up hungover on the set, but no more so than the stuntman. That changed on *Less Than Zero*," he admitted. "For me, the role was like the ghost of Christmas future. The character was an exaggeration of myself. Then things changed and, in some ways, I became an exaggeration of the character."[20]

Sobriety Struggles

By the time Downey wrapped up filming *Less Than Zero*, his substance abuse was beginning to interfere with his career. Downey's manager at the time, Loree Rodkin, convinced him to check himself into a month-long program at a rehabilitation center in Tucson, Arizona. Afterward, he ended up taking a year off from acting to get clean and sober.

Upon returning to work, Downey made his first foray into big-budget action movies with *Air America* in 1990. Costarring Mel Gibson, it follows the adventures of a group of American civilian pilots who fly secret missions in Southeast Asia for the U.S. Central Intelligence Agency (CIA) during the Vietnam War. Downey played Billy Covington, a daring and idealistic young helicopter pilot who is recruited to join the group but grows alarmed by its illegal activities. Despite the star power of Gibson, the movie did poorly with critics and at the box office.

Downey stayed clean while shooting *Air America* in Thailand, but he started using drugs again upon his return to Los Angeles. "He's one of those tortured souls," Parker explained in an interview in 1996. She had decided that she could not put up with the drug use anymore and broke off their relationship in 1991. "You feel so [powerless]. You're always wondering and waiting for a call from someone saying, 'We went to his trailer to get him and he's dead.' I felt so sad and by the end I felt exhausted."[21]

Mel Gibson and Robert Downey Jr. costarred in *Air America*. The two actors would become friends, and Gibson would later become pivotal in helping Downey get his career back on track in the 2000s.

Casting Chaplin

Although he was saddened by the breakup, Downey soon found an exciting new film project to distract him from the problems in his personal life. He learned that the British actor and director Richard Attenborough was planning to make a movie about the life of Charlie Chaplin. Chaplin was a legendary British actor and director known as the original master of slapstick and physical comedy. During the silent film era of the 1920s, he created a lovable character called the Little Tramp, who wobbled around in a ragged, oversized suit with a bowler hat and cane. As the son of a filmmaker, Downey had idolized Chaplin from childhood and felt a connection to his work.

Like many other young actors, Downey recognized that portraying Chaplin had the potential to make him a big star. He wanted the role badly and spent a great deal of time preparing for his audition. He watched Chaplin's films, studied his movements, and worked with a dialect coach to perfect his British accent. Thanks to his intensive preparation, Downey aced his audition. He showed up at his screen test dressed in costume as the Little Tramp and performed an elaborate comedy routine in which he wrestled with a ladder. Attenborough immediately felt that Downey was perfect for the role. It helped that the director wanted to hire a lesser-known actor rather than a big star whom audiences might tend to associate with other roles.

When Attenborough announced his decision to cast Downey, however, the choice proved unpopular on many fronts. Some studio executives wanted a bigger name to play Chaplin in order to sell more tickets to the movie. Others worried Downey's reputation would affect the film. Many fans of the comic legend, meanwhile, felt that only a British actor could do the role of Chaplin justice. Downey was determined to prove the doubters wrong and make his portrayal of Chaplin a career-defining role.

Before filming began, Downey spent six months in intensive study and preparation. He worked with a coach for physical comedy to learn to move like Chaplin. He also printed out photos of Chaplin's expressions and practiced them for hours in front of a mirror. Downey took lessons in order to be able to play tennis and violin left-handed, like Chaplin did. Finally, he visited a film museum in London, England, and convinced the staff to let him try on the actual suit and boots that Chaplin wore as the Little Tramp. By the time shooting started, he was convinced

Downey won over audiences with his portrayal of Charlie Chaplin. Shown here is a scene from *Chaplin,* which also featured actress Marisa Tomei (left).

that he knew more about Chaplin than anyone. "I was so crazy by the end of six and a half months of research that I told Richard Attenborough we needed to rewrite the script because there were too many things that were factually incorrect," he recalled. "They were saying, 'He's going off the deep end.'"[22]

A Remarkable Achievement

Downey's research paid off in an outstanding performance. Even Chaplin's daughter Geraldine, who played a role in the film, said that he captured the spirit of the man perfectly. "It was as if my father came down from heaven and inhabited and possessed him for the length of the movie,"[23] she said. Downey's achievement was all the more remarkable because the film spanned 60 years of Chaplin's life. With the help of state-of-the-art makeup, Downey portrayed the silent film star from his late teens all the way through old age.

As a whole, *Chaplin* received mixed reviews. Some critics disliked the way Attenborough structured the film as a series of flashbacks with an elderly Chaplin looking back over his life. Others complained that the movie focused too much on Chaplin's personal life and failed to give modern audiences a sense of his impact as an actor and filmmaker. Downey's performance in the title role, however, received widespread praise. "He is good and persuasive as the adult Charlie when the material allows, and close to brilliant when he does some of Charlie's early vaudeville and film sketches," Vincent Canby wrote in the *New York Times*. "His slapstick routines are graceful, witty and, most important, really funny."[24] Online reviewer Jeffrey M. Anderson added that "Downey not only imitates Chaplin, but also captures his essence, and the complex joy and sadness that must have come from being the most famous man in the world. He makes you laugh with his effortless slapstick and makes you cry with his heartbreak."[25]

Charlie Chaplin: Master of Mime and Comedy

Charles Spencer Chaplin was born in London on April 16, 1889. Forced to support himself from the age of 10, young Chaplin joined a juvenile theater troupe, honed his performance skills, and became a successful tap dancer and comedian on the London stage.

In 1912, Chaplin expanded his popularity to the United States with a series of vaudeville shows. He signed a motion picture contract and starred in some of the most successful films of the silent era. An innovative master of mime and slapstick comedy, he was best known for creating a disheveled yet gentlemanly character called the Little Tramp.

In 1919, Chaplin joined a group of fellow actors to found United Artists, a film production and distribution company. He won his first Academy Award for the 1928 film *The Circus*, commented on the dehumanizing effects of industrialization in 1936's *Modern Times*, and warned about the rise of Adolf Hitler in *The Great Dictator*, released in 1940. By the time his political views had made him a target of Senator Joseph McCarthy's anti-Communist crusade in the 1950s, Chaplin was one of the biggest celebrities in the world. He died on December 25, 1977.

Award Recognition

Downey put a lot of work into his role as Charlie Chaplin, and this work was acknowledged at award shows throughout

HE SURPASSES HIS UNFOR-
GETTABLE PERFORMANCES IN
THE "GOLD RUSH" AND "CITY
LIGHTS," IN THIS, THE GREATEST
OF ALL HIS GREAT COMEDIES...

Charlie Chaplin

IN

MODERN TIMES

*Written, Directed and
Produced by
CHARLES CHAPLIN*

Released thru
UNITED ARTISTS

Charlie Chaplin was forced to support himself from a young age and went on to become one of the most celebrated comedians of his time. Even in the 21st century, Chaplin is still considered a legend.

1993. He was nominated for the Best Performance by an Actor in a Motion Picture award at the Golden Globe Awards and won a BAFTA Film Award for Best Actor. He was also

The Oscars

Robert Downey Jr. officially broke into the top ranks of his profession in 1993, when he was nominated for a coveted Academy Award for Best Actor in a Leading Role for his performance in *Chaplin*. Known informally as the Oscars, the Academy Awards are the oldest, most prestigious, and most influential form of recognition for outstanding achievement in film. The awards have been presented annually since 1929 by the nonprofit Academy of Motion Picture Arts and Sciences. Oscars are awarded in a number of categories, including Best Picture, Best Director, Best Actor/Actress in a Leading Role, and Best Actor/Actress in a Supporting Role.

Today, the Academy Awards are handed out in February each year during a glamorous ceremony that is watched on television by hundreds of millions of people around the world. Individuals and films that are recognized typically receive a huge boost in media attention and prestige. Even being nominated for an Oscar is considered a tremendous honor. Downey was only 27 years old when he was nominated for his role in *Chaplin*. If he had won, he would have been the youngest Best Actor recipient in the history of the Academy

nominated for the Best Actor in a Leading Role at the Awards Circuit Community Awards and received a nomination at the Chicago Film Critics Association Awards for Best Actor. Downey was even recognized at the London Critics Circle Film Awards, receiving an award for Actor of the Year. He did not, however, win the Academy Award for Best Actor in a Leading Role. Many film industry insiders felt Downey deserved to win, and it was strongly believed that he would

As of 2019, Downey has been nominated for two Academy Awards—the first in 1993 for a leading role in *Chaplin*, and the second for a supporting role in *Tropic Thunder* in 2009.

Awards. Downey earned a second nomination, in the Best Actor in a Supporting Role category, in 2009 for *Tropic Thunder*.

be the one walking away with the award at the end of the night. However, the honor went to Al Pacino.

While some people may have been upset about Downey not winning the award, Downey himself was thrilled to receive this type of recognition at just 27 years old. Downey said, "I felt like I had just knocked one out of the park. I thought, 'You know what? This is the big turning point for me.'"[26] However, after putting so much energy and focus into his work on *Chaplin*, a letdown followed, and Downey returned to partying. He explained, "There was this kind of lull, and I never really found any momentum to focus my creative energy after that, so pretty much expectable things happened."[27] He added, "You'd have thought that at some point I'd sit down and say, 'OK, I just got nominated for *Chaplin*; what I do in the next eighteen months is really key, so maybe I should cut my [marijuana] intake in half and focus on what my plan is.'"[28]

Chapter Three

The Road
to Recovery

In 1992, Downey was receiving acclaim for his role as Charlie Chaplin, and his personal life also changed. Around this time, he met model and aspiring singer Deborah Falconer, and they were married in May, just six weeks after they met. The next year, his life changed even more with three movies and the birth of his son, Indio, on September 7, 1993. Following the acclaim for his role in *Chaplin*, Downey searched for more challenging roles. In 1993, he was in two movies—*Short Cuts* and *Heart and Souls*—and narrated a documentary called *The Last Party*.

"An Amazing Mimic"

In his search for a challenging follow-up to *Chaplin*, Downey appeared in three very different movies over the next year. The most revealing was a feature-length documentary film called *The Last Party*, which chronicled the 1992 presidential race between Democrat Bill Clinton and Republican George H. W. Bush. Although Downey did not have a strong background in politics, he agreed to serve as its on-screen narrator. He traveled the country with a film crew in tow—attending parades, marches, rallies, and both parties' national

Robert Downey Jr. met Deborah Falconer in 1992, and the couple was married shortly thereafter.

conventions—to talk with people about various political issues. Over the course of the movie, however, Downey also talked very candidly about his personal life, including his unusual family background and his parents' divorce. *New York Times* reviewer Stephen Holden wrote that *The Last Party* creates a portrait of "America as a dysfunctional family," adding that this image "plays neatly into Mr. Downey's own personal drama."[29]

Downey also took advantage of an opportunity to work with Robert Altman, an award-winning director known for his experimental and improvisational filmmaking style. He

Downey took a small role in the film *Short Cuts,* directed by award-winning director Robert Altman. He is shown here with some of the cast members of the film.

accepted a small role in Altman's ensemble film *Short Cuts*, which was adapted from a series of interconnected short stories by Raymond Carver. Downey played Bill, a Hollywood makeup artist, and shared screen time with a large cast of well-known actors. The film received positive reviews, with *Variety* describing it as a "complex and full-bodied human comedy."[30]

Downey's biggest acting challenge that year came in his role as the self-absorbed business executive Thomas Reilly in the romantic comedy *Heart and Souls*. The story begins with Thomas's birth in a car that is involved in an accident on its way to the hospital. The accident claims the lives of four strangers (played by Charles Grodin, Kyra Sedgwick, Tom Sizemore, and Alfre Woodard), who end up watching over Thomas as guardian angels throughout his life. When Thomas is 30, the four souls learn that they must use him to achieve their unfulfilled dreams in order to reach heaven. From this point on, the souls take turns inhabiting Thomas's body, with hilarious results. Downey not only plays his own character, he also performs impersonations of the other four actors when their characters take over Thomas's body. Janet Maslin of the *New York Times* called him "an amazing mimic. The best thing about the film is the chance to watch his uncanny impersonations of his co-stars."[31]

An Increasing Impact on a Promising Career

For a while, Downey's substance abuse did not have much impact on his work. By the mid-1990s, however, his addiction began to take a bigger toll on both his career and his personal life. This change occurred when Downey began smoking black-tar heroin.

In 1995, Downey appeared in *Home for the Holidays*, which was a film about a dysfunctional family that gathers for Thanksgiving with funny and heart-wrenching results. He played Tommy Larson, the family's mischievous gay brother.

Although Downey turned in a good performance, he later admitted that he had been high on heroin throughout the filming. His behavior—and his casual attitude about it—bothered director Jodie Foster so much that she wrote him a letter begging him to get help. Convinced that he had the situation under control, Downey ignored Foster's advice.

The problem became more difficult to overlook with Downey's next project, a period drama called *Restoration*, which was also released in 1995. He starred as Robert Merivel, a young doctor whose service to the court of King Charles II results in a series of misadventures. Although

Downey's performance as a doctor in the film *Restoration* was praised by critics. The film takes place in 17th-century England during the Great Plague.

critics praised the quirky charm of Downey's performance in the film, they could not help but notice his behavior during promotional appearances. He often showed up late or abruptly canceled scheduled interviews, for instance.

As time passed, Downey's drug addiction affected his work in increasingly obvious ways. He had started to lose weight and began to look thin, pale, and shaky on camera. This change in appearance was apparent in the film *Hugo Pool*, which was released in 1997 and directed by his father. Downey played an eccentric Dutch filmmaker named Franz Mazur. Although the role called for him to behave strangely, Downey admitted that his bizarre, over-the-top performance was drug induced. Additionally, around this time, critics started to notice that something was wrong with Downey. *Los Angeles Times* reviewer Jack Mathews called it "one of the worst performances he or any major star has recorded on film … Given the actor's off-camera adventures, it's hard not to regard it as the work of someone who's not thinking straight."[32]

A Series of Arrests

Downey's substance abuse also started to cause problems at home during this time. Falconer tried to convince Downey to get clean in order to set a good example for Indio. However, drug addiction, especially to a drug as powerful as heroin, is very hard to recover from. In 1996, Falconer moved out and took Indio with her.

The breakup of his family was hard on Downey, and he became depressed. Additionally, his substance abuse took a greater toll on him. In 1996, Downey was pulled over for speeding and driving erratically on the Pacific Coast Highway near Malibu, California. The police report said that he appeared confused and acted strangely, which convinced the patrolman that he was under the influence of a controlled substance. The police officers searched his car, and Downey was arrested and taken to jail. However, he posted bail and was released later that night.

On July 16—only 10 days before his scheduled court appearance for the first incident—Downey tried to enter what he thought was his home. However, under the influence of drugs and alcohol, he mistakenly entered the home of a neighboring family. Not realizing his error, Downey stumbled into a bedroom and fell asleep on the bed. He was found by the family a short time later, and they called the police to report a stranger in their house. Downey was arrested and charged with being under the influence of a controlled substance and trespassing. Although the second charge was later dropped, Downey was put back in the headlines for his personal struggles rather than his acting talents.

When Downey answered the new charges in court, the judge ordered him to receive inpatient treatment at the Exodus Recovery Center in Marina del Rey, California. Two days later, however, he climbed through a bathroom window at the center and took a taxi to a friend's house. When the police caught up with him, Downey was arrested again for leaving the rehabilitation center in violation of the court order. This time, he remained in jail for several weeks while he awaited further court appearances. Toward the end of July at his next court appearance, Downey told the judge that he recognized the seriousness of his drug addiction and was determined to beat it. The judge responded by sentencing him to several months at a full-time, supervised drug rehabilitation facility, followed by three years' probation and frequent, random drug tests. Downey's many fans hoped that the sentence would enable him to get clean and turn his life around.

Confronting Struggles Through SNL

Downey's personal struggles at the time did not affect his ability to receive roles in movies and TV shows. He received a number of offers during the months he spent in court-ordered drug rehabilitation. In November 1996, for example, he was allowed to leave the rehabilitation facility for a weekend and travel to New York to be the host of an episode

Downey is shown here with Heather Graham (left) and Natasha Wagner (right), his castmates in the film *Two Girls and a Guy*. Downey's performance earned him positive reviews, some of which stated he saved the film.

of *SNL*. He confronted his recent string of misdeeds in a humorous way during his opening monologue. After telling the audience that he brought slides from his summer vacation, Downey proceeded to show images of himself doing things such as accepting a suspicious package and sitting in a jail cell. By poking fun at his problems, Downey seemed to indicate that he would be able to overcome them.

Shortly after Downey was released from the rehabilitation facility in 1997, he starred in a film written and directed by his friend James Toback. *Two Girls and a Guy* tells the story of Blake Allen, a charismatic but self-absorbed actor who is dating two women at the same time. When both of the women show up at his upscale New York City apartment unexpectedly, Allen must face up to his deception. In a review for the *New York Times*, Janet Maslin argued that Downey's performance saved the movie. "Played less winningly, [Allen] could infuriate women and turn men green with envy," she wrote. "Played by Mr. Downey, he's a bristling, clever, volatile one-man show."[33]

Relapse and Rehabilitation

Downey won roles in other high-profile films following his release from rehab. He played a private investigator in *The Gingerbread Man*, which was released in 1998 and based on a John Grisham novel. He also played a Federal Bureau of Investigation (FBI) agent in *U.S. Marshals*, also released in 1998, which was the sequel to the hugely successful 1993 action film *The Fugitive*. However, in September 1997, Downey suffered a relapse and failed a court-ordered drug test. In December, he was back in court for violating the terms of his probation.

Downey apologized for his actions in front of the judge at his court appearance and asked for more time to conquer his addiction. "I've been addicted to drugs in one form or another since I was eight years old,"[34] he explained. His pleas failed to sway the judge. Hoping that a tough stance would scare Downey straight, the judge sentenced him to spend

180 days in prison at the Twin Towers Correctional Facility in Los Angeles. "You need to find out why … you are willing to endure so much pain and turmoil in your life to continue doing drugs," the judge said. "I'm going to send you to jail … I don't care who you are."[35]

Even though the judge sentenced Downey to 180 days, he served only 113 of them. During this time, Downey spent most of his time reading in his cell. He was allowed to watch TV for an hour each day and take a shower twice a week. Although he was permitted to have visitors, Downey refused to see anyone. Finally, on March 31, 1998, Downey was released from jail and went directly to a live-in rehabilitation center, where he remained until August. When Downey finally emerged, having completed his sentence, many people close to him hoped that the experience would help him turn his life around. His attorney said, "I can't say, and no one can, that Robert will succeed. But I can say, based on the dozens of conversations I've had with him, that he really does want to stay sober."[36]

New Determination

Downey succeeded in his personal battle against drug addiction for about nine months. During this period of sobriety, he shot the critically acclaimed movie *Wonder Boys*, which was released in 2000. Downey played Terry Crabtree, a book editor who makes a visit to a college town to encourage a frustrated English professor to finish his long-awaited novel. As usual, Downey received positive reviews for his performance. Offscreen, however, he continued to experience problems in his personal life. Legal bills depleted his savings, and the Internal Revenue Service (IRS) placed a lien on his house for unpaid taxes.

In the face of mounting pressures, Downey started using drugs again in the spring of 1999. "I found myself not having my priorities straight and I relapsed,"[37] he noted. He skipped court-ordered drug tests in violation of his probation, and he was forced to undergo a psychiatric evaluation. When he appeared in court in August, Downey admitted that his addiction was out of control. The judge responded by issuing an even harsher sentence than before. Downey's 3-year probation was revoked, and he was sentenced to spend that amount of time—less 201 days he had already served—at the California Substance Abuse Treatment Facility and State Prison in Corcoran.

Downey spent the next year sharing a medium-security cell with four other inmates. He worked in the kitchen at the facility for wages of 8 cents an hour and sang in the prison chorus. He also took the General Educational Development exam to earn his high school equivalency diploma. This time, Downey accepted visitors, viewing it as an opportunity to reconnect with his family and friends. Although he tried to make the best of the situation, he recognized that being in prison forced him to miss out on many things. "Watching the Oscars from jail was a trip, a real trip," he acknowledged. "But, you know, people are people. I wasn't thinking about my own tragic situation. I was going, 'I didn't expect her to win. Isn't that nice?' I was just [an average person] watching it, you know?"[38]

In August 2000, Downey was released from prison. His freedom came earlier than expected because his lawyers convinced the court to give him additional credit for the time he had already served. Still, spending that time in prison made an impact on Downey. Describing the experience as "awful" and "horrible,"[39] he left prison determined to straighten himself out and avoid going back. He checked himself into Walden House, a residential drug treatment facility in Los Angeles, to continue the hard work of recovery. "Addiction is addiction and I'm an addict who has to fight for the rest of his life against the allure of substance abuse," he explained. "Every day that I'm clean is a step in the right direction. But every day poses a risk that I can fall back and Hollywood is a palace of temptation. So I'm waging my fight against that backdrop, but I feel good about my life right now."[40]

An Uncomfortable Interview

In 2015, Downey walked out of an interview with Krishnan Guru-Murthy while promoting *Avengers: Age of Ultron*, which was immediately widely talked about in articles and tabloids. The interview was supposed to be about the new movie. However, the interviewer repeatedly asked Downey about his personal life, even when Downey pointed out that his life was not the point of the interview. He felt uncomfortable with and surprised by the interviewer's line of questioning. In another interview the week after, he stated that he wished he had walked out of the interview sooner. Downey said, "I'm one of those guys where I'm always kind of assuming the social decorum is in play and that we're promoting a superhero movie, a lot of kids are going to see it … This has nothing to do with your … dark agenda that I'm feeling like all of a sudden ashamed and obligated to accommodate your [interests]."[1]

Drug and alcohol addiction are highly stigmatized disorders with a lot of judgment surrounding them. It is extremely hard for people to admit to a current or

Ally McBeal

Despite taking a year off from acting, Downey still had many friends in Hollywood who were eager to see him back at work. However, even though many people respected his talent, some were reluctant to take the risk of hiring him. If he suffered another relapse and returned to prison, it could cause a costly disruption in production or even force the previous addiction because "they have little to gain and everything to lose."[2] When someone such as Robert Downey Jr. is in the public eye and their personal struggles are the subjects of headlines, many people already know about this past and want to talk about it. This line of questioning about addictions, whether with someone in the public eye or an average person, can make the person feel incredibly uncomfortable and alone. Additionally, this judgment and the feelings that result from it can cause a person to turn back to the substance that they were addicted to in an effort to make themselves feel better. As Sovereign Health Treatment Centers wrote, "For this reason, the best thing people can do for recovered addicts is to let them know that they accept them and understand that they've suffered. They should also do what they can to accommodate the recovered addict's needs."[3]

1. Quoted in Hilary Lewis, "Robert Downey Jr. Opens Up About Interview Walkout: 'This Has Nothing to Do with Your Creepy, Dark Agenda,'" *Hollywood Reporter*, April 28, 2015. www.hollywoodreporter.com/heat-vision/robert-downey-jr-opens-up-792009.

2. Courtney Lopresti, "10 Things to Never Say to a Recovering Addict," Sovereign Health Treatment Centers, June 8, 2015. www.sovhealth.com/alcohol-abuse/10-things-never-say-recovering-addict/.

3. Lopresti, "10 Things to Never Say to a Recovering Addict."

cancellation of a film project. The companies that provided insurance to the major film studios refused to cover Downey for this reason. Despite this, a few people believed in him enough to give him a chance. One of these supporters was David E. Kelley, the writer and producer of hit TV series such as *L.A. Law*, *Chicago Hope*, *Picket Fences*, and *The Practice*.

Kelley offered Downey a role on his successful legal comedy-drama *Ally McBeal*. Downey played an attorney,

Robert Downey Jr. and Calista Flockhart are shown here arriving at the Golden Globe Awards. Downey and Flockhart costarred in *Ally McBeal*, and Downey won a Golden Globe Award for his work on the show.

Larry Paul, who emerges as an important new love interest for the main character, who was played by Calista Flockhart. He brought his considerable energy and charm to the role and developed great on-screen chemistry with Flockhart. In fact, many reviewers credited his addition to the cast with revitalizing the show, which was widely believed to have lost its creative focus. Downey's impressive comeback received extensive coverage in the press, and many fans hoped that the actor had beaten his addiction once and for all.

However, around this time, Deborah Falconer officially filed for divorce after more than four years of separation, and Downey's recovery faltered again. Downey became depressed and returned to using drugs. "It was my lowest point in terms of addictions," he acknowledges. "At that stage, I didn't [care] whether I ever acted again."[41] He was arrested at a Palm Springs resort over Thanksgiving for possession of cocaine, though he remained free on bail while the case wound its way through the courts.

In January 2001, Downey's performance in *Ally McBeal* was recognized with a Golden Globe Award for Best Performance by an Actor in a Supporting Role in a Series, Mini-Series, or Motion Picture Made for Television. A few months after he accepted the award, though, Downey got arrested again. A police officer saw him trying to buy drugs in an alley on the west side of Los Angeles on April 24, 2001, and determined that he was under the influence of a controlled substance. It turned out to be the last straw for Kelley. He fired Downey and wrote his character out of *Ally McBeal*. "We are wrapping up the stories for the final few episodes for the season without him," Kelley's production company said in a statement. "Robert is a unique talent and a very special person, and we wish him the best and hope for his full recovery."[42]

Proposition 36

In November 2000, California passed the Substance Abuse and Crime Prevention Act, also known as Proposition 36. This "initiative allows first and second time non-violent,

Insurance Policies and the Entertainment Industry

As Downey struggled to overcome drug addiction and legal problems, he found it difficult to land acting jobs. Part of the problem was that he was unable to get insurance.

Producing a movie or TV show is time-consuming and expensive. There is always a risk that some unforeseen problem could interrupt, postpone, or even cancel a project while it is in production. For example, an actor could break both arms during production, as Jeremy Renner did on the set of the film *Tag*, or a storm could destroy a set or damage equipment.

Before any film project gets approved, therefore, production companies take out insurance policies to protect their investment and compensate them for financial losses. These insurance policies cover cast members, camera operators, producers, and other key people whose injury, illness, or death would disrupt filming. Insurance companies often require these individuals to undergo medical examinations or submit health histories before they provide coverage. If an actor has a history of substance abuse, insurance companies consider them to pose a high risk and often deny coverage.

simple drug possession offenders the opportunity to receive substance abuse treatment instead of incarceration."[43] This initiative was put into effect in 2001, so when Downey's latest cases went to trial, he was able to receive treatment instead of a prison sentence. The judge sentenced Downey to one year at Wavelengths International, a residential drug rehabilitation facility. Following his time at Wavelengths, he would be on probation for three years and would be randomly drug tested. However, if Downey was arrested again and broke the terms of Proposition 36, he would face up to four years in prison. It was this treatment at Wavelengths International that helped Downey remain clean and sober.

Chapter **Four**

Making
a Comeback

Downey completed his yearlong program at Wavelengths International in 2002. Citing July 4, 2002, as the date of his recovery, he said, "The country's independence, my independence."[44] In order to make the full recovery that he was committed to, Downey took up a 12-step recovery program, yoga, meditation, and martial arts, in particular, the Wing Chun form of martial arts.

To give him the focus and routine to keep him clean and sober, Downey sought out Eric Oram, founder of the L.A. Wing Chun Academy. In an interview on *The Oprah Winfrey Show*, Downey said, "Martial has been … I can't even say how much it's impacted my ability to stay well and focused … It's a spiritual practice. It's grounded me and its primary purpose is to promote a sense of spiritual warriordom and to respect your society and to be prepared to defend yourself and your society if necessary."[45]

Downey took up yoga and meditation to help him avoid temptation and achieve emotional balance. He switched to a diet of natural and whole foods, and he traveled with a massage therapist and an herbalist, both of whom also contributed to his well-being. "Once you have that support," Downey said, "why would you fare as well without it? It's

Downey took up Wing Chun shortly after leaving Wavelengths International. He is shown here practicing this form of martial arts.

Fight Choreography

Robert Downey Jr. gives some of the credit for his recovery from drug addiction to his discovery of Wing Chun kung fu. Wing Chun is a Chinese martial art that teaches practitioners techniques of self-defense and close combat.

The discipline of Wing Chun emphasizes biomechanics—body structure, positioning, and balance—rather than brute strength. Practitioners are supposed to be firm but flexible, like bamboo. In addition to physical conditioning, the martial art gives practitioners a sense of well-being and spiritual calm.

Downey sought out L.A. Wing Chun Academy founder Eric Oram to train him in the martial art form, and Downey would end up incorporating skills from Wing Chun into his stunts in movies such as *Iron Man* and *Sherlock Holmes*. Oram said,

Film fight choreography has its own demands ... it's focus, control, timing, and lots of repetition. It's remembering where you are every step of the way in telling a story and yet playing it as if it's happening for the first time live. There's an art to that, and Robert works very, very hard in that process. I've fight doubled him for minor stuff, like pick-up shots, but Robert does all his own stuff when it comes to fights. When the camera's on him, it's really him doing it.[1]

However, Downey has recently started to stray away from performing some of these stunts, allowing the stuntmen on set to step in.

1. Quoted in Sam Dehority, "Robert Downey Jr.: 'He Was Skinny,'" *Men's Journal*, accessed on August 14, 2018. www.mensjournal.com/health-fitness/robert-downey-jr-he-was-skinny/.

like, you know, if you become a more effective engine, you need more maintenance."[46]

Turning the Corner in Recovery

Once he had the support he needed, Downey felt confident that he had turned the corner in his recovery from drug addiction. He found it difficult to convince people in Hollywood that he would be able to stay clean this time, however. "The hard thing is going to be convincing people who are putting up huge sums of money that there's not going to be any problems,"[47] said producer Mark Burg, who had worked with Downey on *The Gingerbread Man*. Insurance played a big part in the hesitation surrounding casting Downey in film projects. Downey had gone through so many personal struggles that the insurance companies refused to cover him.

Downey found himself in a tough situation. He could not work as an actor without insurance, and he could not get insurance without proving that he was a reliable actor. He needed help to break back in to the acting business. It came from his friend Mel Gibson, who had worked with Downey on *Air America* and had experienced his own problems with alcohol abuse. Gibson offered Downey the starring role in a new film he was producing called *The Singing Detective*, which was released in 2003. He also agreed to pay for Downey's insurance policy out of his own pocket.

Based on a popular British TV series, *The Singing Detective* told the story of Dan Dark, a writer of detective novels who suffers from a painful and debilitating skin condition. Stuck in a hospital bed, Dark imagines an elaborate fantasy life in which he sings, dances, and solves mysteries. The role required Downey to act beneath grotesque, rubbery makeup in the hospital scenes, as well as to showcase his musical talents in the fantasy sequences.

"I don't know who else could have done it," said director Keith Gordon. "From the darkest depths to the silly comedy to the singing and dancing, Robert has that ability to change gears emotionally."[48] Although *The*

Singing Detective was a flop at the box office, it provided critics with a vivid reminder of Downey's wide-ranging abilities. With Gibson vouching for him, it also gave the actor a valuable foothold to climb back into the film industry.

Downey is shown here signing autographs for fans at *The Singing Detective* premiere at the Toronto International Film Festival.

Finding Love with Susan Levin

A string of new projects followed quickly for the actor, including a role in the thriller *Gothika*, which was released in 2003. Downey played a psychiatrist who treats a woman who is accused of murdering her husband but has no memory of committing the crime. Although the film was poorly received by critics, making it turned out to have a tremendous impact on Downey's life. Downey was romantically interested in one of *Gothika*'s producers, Susan Levin, right away. However, she thought he was strange and rejected his advances. He persisted, though, and Levin finally agreed to go out with him after they finished shooting the movie.

After Downey and Levin had dated for about six months, he proposed marriage on November 6, 2003—her 30th birthday. She accepted with the stipulation that he must remain clean and sober. "She's been very firm that if he's going to be with her, he has to really toe the line,"[49] said Joel Silver, one of the producers on *Gothika*. Downey eagerly agreed to the terms. His divorce from Deborah Falconer was finalized in the spring of 2004, and he exchanged vows with Levin on August 27, 2005, at the Windy Dunes estate in upstate New York. Downey claims that his second marriage gave him a sense of happiness, fulfillment, and contentment that helped him move beyond his earlier problems. "I'm not the poster boy for anything anymore," he stated. "I don't ... relate to that time in my life. Because it is something that I transcended, somehow, with really a lot of ... love and support."[50]

With Levin's encouragement, Downey found a new outlet for his creative energies. He recorded an album of music. "My vice, it seems now, is creativity," he said. "It's all about living a normal, balanced life."[51] Downey had taught himself to play the piano as a boy, and he always took a keyboard with him on film locations to help him relax and unwind. Over the years, he had composed a number of songs about his experiences and interests. Downey first came to public attention as a singer and musician during his stint on *Ally McBeal*. His character, Larry Paul, often played the piano and sang on the show. Downey's musical interludes were so

Downey met Susan Levin on the set of *Gothika,* and they started dating after filming ended. They married in 2005 and are still together as of 2019.

popular with fans of the show that he ended up performing several songs on the *Ally McBeal* soundtrack album.

Downey's own album, *The Futurist*, which was released in 2004, consists of eight original songs plus a couple of covers, including Charlie Chaplin's famous ballad "Smile." All the tracks showcase Downey's voice against spare, jazzy arrangements featuring him on the piano. Although the album received mediocre reviews, Downey's many fans snapped up copies anyway. Downey is proud of *The Futurist*, even though he recognizes that his fame as a troubled actor created the opportunity for him to record it. "No way would I ever get to express myself musically if I wasn't an actor of ill repute," he acknowledged. "You don't get on 'Oprah' if you live a gleaming life and then just happen to cross over into music."[52]

Rebuilding a Reputation

As more time passed without Downey suffering a relapse, he slowly managed to rebuild his reputation. He churned out solid performances in 10 films between 2005 and 2007. For example, in 2005, Downey played reporter Joe Wershba in *Good Night, and Good Luck*, the critically acclaimed biography of legendary journalist Edward R. Murrow. He also ventured into family comedy, portraying the sinister animal researcher Dr. Kozak in Disney's *The Shaggy Dog*, which was released in 2006. In 2007, Downey starred as a high school principal who matches wits with a new student in *Charlie Bartlett*. This same year, he also starred in a movie that was based on real-life events that occurred in the late 1960s and early 1970s. During this time, the Zodiac Killer murdered 5 people, injured 2 others, and claimed to have killed as many as 37 people. The Zodiac Killer was never found, and the case remains a mystery. The case is even more bothersome because the killer sent letters to journalists about the murders and included ciphers, or codes, that would allegedly lead to his identity. Journalist Paul Avery was one of those people who received letters from the Zodiac Killer, one of which threatened him. In *Zodiac*, which details the hunt for

Robert and Susan Downey

Robert Downey Jr. found happiness and contentment with his second wife, Susan. Susan Levin was born in Chicago, Illinois, on November 6, 1973. She was determined to make a career in the film industry from the age of 12. After graduating as valedictorian from Schaumburg High School in Illinois, she earned a bachelor's degree from the University of Southern California's School of Cinema and Television.

In 1995, Levin took a job with New Line Cinema, where she did uncredited production work on the *Mortal Kombat* series of martial arts movies. In 1999, she moved to Silver Pictures, a production company owned by Joel Silver. In 2002, Levin received her first full-credit producer job on the thriller *Gothika*, where she met and began dating her future husband.

Levin married Robert Downey Jr. on August 27, 2005. The spouses enjoyed working together on such films as *Kiss Kiss Bang Bang*, *Sherlock Holmes*, and *Iron Man 2*. In 2009, Susan Downey left Silver Pictures to launch a new production company, Team Downey, to develop film projects in conjunction with her husband. In 2012, their family expanded with the addition of son Exton Elias, and expanded again in 2014 with the birth of daughter Avri Roel.

Susan Downey wanted to be in the film industry from a young age and pursued it tirelessly through her schooling and production work. Susan and Robert are shown here at a 2007 Oscar party.

the Zodiac Killer during this time, Downey played Avery, and the film as well as Downey received positive reviews.

The *New York Times* stated, "The story structure is as intricate as the storytelling is seamless."[53] Although most of the films

Downey is shown here with fellow *Zodiac* actors Mark Ruffalo and Chloë Sevigny.

Downey made during this period received decent reviews and performed respectably at the box office, none of them became a huge hit.

Downey had especially high hopes for *Kiss Kiss Bang Bang*, which was released in 2005. Downey played Harry Lockhart, a small-time New York thief who stumbles into an acting audition while running from the police. He ends up landing the part by giving a moving speech about the perils of a life of crime. The filmmakers send Lockhart to Hollywood, where he teams up with a Los Angeles police officer (played by Val Kilmer) to research his role as a thief. Critics praised

Val Kilmer and Robert Downey Jr. are shown here at the *Kiss Kiss Bang Bang* premiere.

Kiss Kiss Bang Bang for its combination of stylized action and dark humor, but—to Downey's great disappointment—it did not last long in movie theaters. "It was going to be my ... emergence into 21st-century cinema," he said. "When it tanked, I was heartbroken."[54]

Kiss Kiss Bang Bang was still notable, though, because it featured the acting debut of Downey's son, Indio, as a younger version of Lockhart. Indio enjoyed working with his dad, but he quickly abandoned acting in favor of music and started a band with some friends. A major benefit of Downey's new, stable lifestyle was that it gave him the opportunity to spend more time with his son, and Indio often came to visit him and Susan. Downey appreciated how far he had come to achieve a normal family life.

The only thing missing from Downey's life—and the one thing that could cement his career resurgence—was a starring role in a blockbuster movie. As a successful producer, Susan Downey knew how important box office success could be for an actor's future prospects. She also realized that, despite his many gifts, her husband had yet to appear in a smash-hit film during his three-plus decade career in show business. As Downey's reputation steadily improved, he and his wife began looking for a mainstream film project that could launch him to the next level of stardom.

Chapter **Five**

"I Am Iron Man"

For years, Downey struggled to rebuild his reputation in Hollywood. The 1990s were an especially tough time, and it built to the point where he was not cast in projects because he could not get insured. Downey's rise from this point to the center of a major movie franchise is remarkable and an inspiration to those who are also struggling with personal issues such as drug addiction. In a 2008 interview with *Entertainment Weekly*, Downey said, "Why am I having this year? ... To tell you the truth, I haven't fully digested what's happened to me before, during, and after *Iron Man* ... But I do know that I don't want to waste any more time. That's why I'm putting my nose to the grindstone. That's why I'm cranking them out."[55] Downey's role as Tony Stark/Iron Man in the MCU not only catapulted him into a new level of superstardom, but it also brought new life to a struggling comics company.

The Marvel Universe

Today, Marvel is a widely known name with an extremely successful series of movies, but for a while, the company was struggling. The history of Marvel goes back to 1939. At that point, Detective Comics (later known as DC Comics) had already published *Action Comics* number 1 in 1938, which featured the first Superman story. To capitalize on the new popularity of comics (which only began to take shape around 1933), magazine publisher Martin Goodman started Timely Comics.

Timely's first issue, *Marvel Comics* number 1, arrived in October 1939. "Marvel" was a word that would stick with Goodman throughout the years—Timely Comics is the precursor to Marvel Comics, and many superheroes were introduced through these early years. Nearly two years after the beginning of Timely Comics, one of Marvel's primary superheroes was introduced. The first Captain America comic was published in March 1941 and featured him fighting Adolf Hitler on the cover—this same cover is on the comics being bought by the children in a scene in *Captain America: The First Avenger*. Hitler and World War II were themes of early Timely Comics because World War II was being fought at the time. In fact, when Captain America fought Hitler on the cover of *Captain America Comics* number 1, the United States had not even entered the war yet. From the start, Timely Comics incorporated real-world settings and current events into their story lines. Later, especially in the character of Tony Stark/Iron Man, real-world science and technologies would also be incorporated.

However, as World War II ended in 1945 and the 1940s drew to a close, the popularity of comics dropped, and Timely canceled its line of comics in 1950. The next year, Goodman started Atlas Comics. Atlas briefly tried to bring back superheroes, but their focus was on other genres. In 1956, DC Comics experienced success with reintroducing superhero titles, and in the early 1960s, Atlas changed its name to Marvel Comics. In 1961, writer Stan Lee and artist and writer Jack Kirby were tasked with creating a superhero team to rival that of DC's Justice League (the combination of popular characters such as Superman, Batman, and Wonder Woman), and thus the Marvel Universe was born.

The universe started with the Fantastic Four and took place in the real world, just like the early years of Timely Comics. Lee and Kirby also tried to make their characters more

Stan Lee (right) was responsible for the creation of hundreds of characters and superhero teams, including the Avengers. He is shown here with Marvel Studios president Kevin Feige.

lifelike and original by having them interact in realistic ways. Following the Fantastic Four, more characters were introduced throughout the early 1960s, including Spider-Man, the X-Men, the Hulk, and Iron Man, who was introduced in 1963. Building

Iron Man was introduced in 1963 in *Tales of Suspense* number 39, shown here.

these characters and their stories in such realistic ways gained Marvel a larger following and built up its reputation. The stories confronted issues such as race relations, drug abuse, and alcohol abuse. In 1978, Tony Stark started to show signs of alcohol abuse in the comics, which adds even more depth to Downey's portrayal of the character in the MCU.

Marvel and DC have been the top comic publishers for decades with DC rising to prominence in the 1980s. However, in the 1990s, the comics industry started to collapse, and in 1996, Marvel filed for bankruptcy. The company was salvaged the following year and merged with the company Toy Biz. Unfortunately, throughout this time, the film rights to some of the most popular characters were given to a variety of movie studios. Film rights for the Hulk were given to Paramount; Sony acquired Spider-Man; and 21st Century Fox acquired X-Men, Daredevil, and the Fantastic Four.

However, the film rights to Iron Man bounced between studios, starting out at 21st Century Fox, switching to New Line Cinema, then bouncing back to Marvel. This proved to be an incredibly fortunate event for Marvel. David Maisel, the chief operating officer of Marvel Studios at the time, "secured a revolving line of credit to the tune of $525 million from Merrill Lynch to produce up to 10 movies based on characters that Marvel still owned the film rights to. When *Iron Man* came back into the fold in November 2005, it was announced as the first film in the revamped and relaunched Marvel Studios, which would act as an independent studio."[56] With this new beginning for Iron Man, all previous scripts were tossed, and Jon Favreau was hired as director. Kevin Feige, president of Marvel Studios, was producer on the movie.

Casting Iron Man

Once Iron Man was back with Marvel Studios and the plan was set up for a series of superhero movies, casting the role of Tony Stark/Iron Man became a new problem. Feige was underwhelmed by the initial list of potential Tony Starks that the casting director sent to him. While meeting with Feige,

The Arc Reactor

Russell Bobbitt is property master and head of props at Marvel. This means he is responsible for providing and creating anything that the actors will touch in MCU films. He has been behind some of the most recognizable and iconic props in the MCU, such as Thor's hammer Mjölnir and Captain America's shield. Additionally, sometimes the prop masters end up creating props that they do not know the significance of at the time. For example, when Bobbitt was working on the first *Thor* movie, which was released in 2011, Kevin Feige asked him to create a small gauntlet that would be seen quickly in the background of a shot in *Thor*—this gauntlet was the Infinity Gauntlet, which would be the focus of *Avengers: Infinity War* in 2018. However, the most challenging task for him involved Tony Stark's miniaturized arc reactor early in *Iron Man*. This miniaturized arc reactor in his chest keeps the shrapnel in his body from entering his heart and killing him. Stark builds his first one when he is held hostage in a cave, and it was this cave scene that was the greatest challenge for Bobbitt. Bobbitt said, "I taught him how wiring works. He soldered and we have

Favreau suddenly said Downey's name as a potential actor to play Iron Man. Feige thought it was an interesting idea, but they dismissed it. However, the idea never truly left. When Downey's name was thrown around even more as a possibility for Iron Man, certain people fought against the idea of him in such a prominent role that was not only the first solo movie from Marvel Studios, but also would launch a series of movies based around a roster of superheroes. Feige said, "There were people in our company who directly said, 'No. You can't [cast

these extreme close up shots and it really defined Iron Man in that moment."[1] The reason why Downey had to learn how to solder properly is because with how close the shot was, it was not something that could be faked—he needed to believably pull off the scene, which meant learning how wiring works.

1. Quoted in Nick Evans, "The Hardest Scene Marvel's Propmaster Has Ever Worked On Involved Robert Downey Jr.," Cinema Blend, accessed on August 15, 2018. www.cinemablend.com/news/2438189/the-hardest-scene-marvels-propmaster-has-ever-worked-on-involved-robert-downey-jr.

Fans often dress up as MCU characters at comic conventions. The miniaturized arc reactor is an important part of this costume, as seen on the fan shown here.

Downey]."[57] Feige and Favreau simultaneously were looking for alternatives while still trying to push Downey into the role. According to the *Los Angeles Times*, "They called the insurance companies, which had no problems with Downey anymore because he'd been clean for five years. They called colleagues who vouched for him. The filmmakers pointed out that even the family-friendly giant Walt Disney had no problem putting Downey in 'The Shaggy Dog.'"[58]

Following this, it came down to Downey screen testing for

Elon Musk

When Jon Favreau was bringing the story of Iron Man from the comics to the big screen, he struggled with making Tony Stark feel like a real person. When Stan Lee created Tony Stark's character in the 1960s, he was inspired by Howard Hughes. Hughes lived from 1905 to 1976 and was an inventor and aviator, and he also produced and directed films. Hughes became wealthy and was a well-known celebrity, but he was also known to be reclusive and eccentric. When *Iron Man* was being filmed in early 2007, Favreau used a building complex that was previously owned by Hughes Aircraft, which was a defense and aerospace contractor started by the inventor.

In the early 2000s, when Favreau, Downey, and others were making *Iron Man*, they needed a modern spin on the character to make him connect to moviegoers and Marvel fans today. Downey suggested they meet with Elon Musk, an investor and engineer who cofounded PayPal and formed SpaceX—a company that makes spacecraft. Additionally, Musk is chief executive officer of and one of the first investors in the electric car company Tesla. The SpaceX facilities were not far from where *Iron Man* was being filmed, and Downey went to meet with Musk and received a personal tour. When Downey returned to the *Iron Man* set, he "asked that Favreau be sure to place a Tesla Roadster in Tony Stark's workshop. 'After meeting

the role. Favreau said, "Once we rolled the camera it was inarguable. There was nobody who could say he was not Iron Man."[59] Susan Downey recalled, "He really, really wanted it … Other than Chaplin, it's the role he's gone after the hardest. He knew he could do it, and he knew he had to prove it to people."[60] Robert added,

Elon and making him real to me, I felt like having his presence in the workshop,' Downey said. 'They became contemporaries. Elon was someone Tony probably hung out with and partied with, or more likely they went on some weird jungle trek together.'[1] Musk later made a cameo in *Iron Man 2*, which was released in 2010.

1. Quoted in Ashlee Vance, "Elon Musk's Space Dream Almost Killed Tesla," *Bloomberg*, May 14, 2015. www.bloomberg.com/graphics/2015-elon-musk-spacex/.

Elon Musk was an inspiration for the character of Tony Stark in *Iron Man* and would later make an appearance in *Iron Man 2*.

Why am I the guy for this job? Because the story is the most duplicitous and conflicted of all the Marvel characters, because he's really just a guy who gets put in an extraordinary set of circumstances—partially due to his own character defects and partially due to his lineage—and you can pick a

million Joseph Campbell myths and look them up, but none
of them apply more to me, and there's nothing I could bring
more to than this job and this story.[61]

Even though studio executives were pushing him to consider younger, lesser-known actors, the director became convinced that Downey's life experiences made him perfect for the role. "Tony Stark goes through a bit of a moral reawakening in this movie," Favreau explained. "You can't have a moral reawakening if you're in high school. You have to have done things in your life to be able to look back and say that I've made mistakes or maybe I should reevaluate the way I approach things."[62] The combination of multiple elements, including casting Downey as Tony Stark/Iron Man, proved to be successful for Marvel and turned Downey into a box office superstar. In its opening weekend, *Iron Man* earned more than $98 million. Throughout its run at the box office, it made more than $318 million in the United States and more than $585 million worldwide. This was even more remarkable because Iron Man was a comic character that many people had never heard of. If the movie completely failed at the box office, the MCU would have looked very different—or possibly would not exist at all. In particular, one line in the movie completely changed the MCU going forward. At the end of the film, in a press conference, Tony Stark says the line, "I am Iron Man."[63] This line was not in the script and was improvised by Downey while filming. The admission surprised and excited Feige, and he chose to leave it in the final cut. In the comics, it takes many years for Stark to admit to the fact that he is Iron Man. Feige said in a 2018 interview on the 10th anniversary of *Iron Man*,

That success inspired us to go further in … trusting ourselves
to find balance of staying true to the comics and the spirit
of the comics but not being afraid to adapt and evolve and
change things …

It's a fine line … If you're changing something for no reason, that's one thing, but if you're changing something because you want to double-down on the spirit of who the character is? That's a change we'll make. Tony Stark not reading off the card and not sticking with the fixed story? Him just blurting out "I am Iron Man?" That seems very much in keeping with who that character is …

I think it did inspire us on all the movies … what I love now—20 movies in—is how fans expect the MCU to change and adapt. They expect us to be inspired by the comics as opposed to being slavishly devoted to them.[64]

Many fans and Hollywood insiders also felt pleased to see Downey achieve the success he had long deserved. "To have another shot at this, after what he's had and lost, is as redemptive a story as the movie itself,"[65] Favreau said.

Tropic Thunder *and* The Soloist

While Downey was shooting *Iron Man*, actor and director Ben Stiller approached him about an intriguing new film project called *Tropic Thunder*. Stiller first came up with the premise for the film in the 1980s—a time when Hollywood churned out numerous movies set during the Vietnam War. Some of Stiller's actor friends went to U.S. military boot camps to prepare for their roles in these films. He started thinking about what would happen if a group of actors thought they were shooting a big-budget war movie but mistakenly got involved in an actual war. Stiller explored this theme in the dark comedy *Tropic Thunder*, which he wrote, directed, and costarred in.

Downey traveled to Hawai'i to begin shooting *Tropic Thunder* just two weeks after he wrapped up *Iron Man*. Stiller asked Downey to play the role of Kirk Lazarus, a five-time Academy Award–winning Australian actor who takes his work very seriously. Lazarus's motivation throughout the movie is to win an Academy Award, and ironically, it was *Tropic Thunder* that earned Downey his second Academy Award nomination.

Downey lined up his next major film project while he was on location shooting *Tropic Thunder*. British filmmaker Joe Wright showed up on the set and told Downey about a movie he was going to be working on called *The Soloist*. As Downey said, "He tells me this story about friendship and faith. All of a sudden I start feeling all my old theater heartstrings being pulled. Before Joe left the island, I knew I'd be doing *The Soloist*."[66] *The Soloist* is based on the true story of Steve Lopez and Nathaniel Ayers. Downey played Lopez, a newspaper columnist who discovers that a homeless man he meets on the streets of Los Angeles, Nathaniel Ayers, is actually a classically trained musician. Ayers was training at Juilliard's music program but then left because of his struggles with schizophrenia. As Lopez tries to help Ayers find a place to live and reconnect with his musical talents as well as receive treatment for his schizophrenia, Lopez also raises awareness of the larger problem of homelessness. "*The Soloist* wouldn't work half as

Robert Downey Jr. and the Legend of the Hidden Food

In 2012's *The Avengers*, fans noticed Downey was always eating. Throughout filming the movie, Downey brought his own food to the set, hid it, and would occasionally take it out to eat while filming a scene. The crew could not always find Downey's hidden food to remove it, so they eventually just let it be and let his snacking scenes stay in the movie. Plus, these scenes also provided comedic relief, such as one moment in which Tony Stark offers Steve Rogers/Captain America a blueberry.

well without Mr. Downey's astringent, bristly take on a man whose best intentions eventually collide with difficult truths," reviewer Manohla Dargis wrote in the *New York Times*. "The actor is a wonder."[67]

Sherlock Holmes

Downey's remarkable string of hit movies continued with the 2009 release of *Sherlock Holmes*, based on Sir Arthur Conan Doyle's famous series of novels about a brilliant British detective. Director Guy Ritchie planned to update the traditional detective story by turning Sherlock Holmes into a tough guy who competes in boxing matches and sword fights. Susan Downey signed on as a producer and encouraged her husband to take on the role. "She said that when you read the description of the guy—quirky and kind of nuts—it could be a description of me," Downey noted. "When he feels he's not inspired or motivated by some creative charge, he'll fall into a state where he barely speaks a word for three days, and when he's engaged, he has incredible amounts of energy, super-human energy."[68]

When the action-packed *Sherlock Holmes* was released on Christmas Day 2009, it broke the single-day box office record for the holiday by earning $25 million. It went on to reach the $100 million mark during its first week in theaters, making Downey the star of a second blockbuster movie franchise. Although the overall film received mixed reviews, many critics praised Downey's on-screen chemistry with Jude Law, who played Holmes's assistant, Dr. Watson. Downey also won a Golden Globe Award in 2010 for Best Performance by an Actor in a Motion Picture—Musical or Comedy for his performance. "It seems impossible now that anybody other than Robert could have played him," Ritchie said. "He thinks like Sherlock Holmes, he's complicated like Sherlock Holmes, and he can really brawl."[69]

Shortly after he finished shooting *Sherlock Holmes*, Downey went back to work on a sequel to *Iron Man*. In *Iron Man 2*, released in 2010, Tony Stark faces off against an evil Russian

In 2009, Robert Downey Jr. launched another major film franchise with *Sherlock Holmes*. Downey plays the title character while Jude Law (left) plays his assistant, Dr. Watson.

physicist (played by Mickey Rourke) and races against time to fix his failing miniature arc reactor in his chest. Although the second installment in the franchise did not receive as favorable reviews as the first one, Downey's performance earned a great deal of praise. Like its predecessor, *Iron Man 2* was a huge success at the box office, earning more than $623 million worldwide. *Iron Man 2* proved that the first movie in the series and the MCU as a whole were not flukes and were here to stay.

Following the success of *Iron Man*, blockbusters starring Downey were released nearly every year. As a proven box office draw, Downey had his choice of lucrative future

Sherlock Adaptations

Robert Downey Jr. jumped at the chance to portray one of the most famous characters in all of literature on the big screen. Sherlock Holmes was created by Scottish author Sir Arthur Conan Doyle in 1887. The fictional detective went on to appear in four novels and more than fifty short stories over the next four decades. Most of the tales are narrated by Holmes's trusted friend and assistant, Dr. John Watson.

As presented in Doyle's stories, Holmes is a brilliant detective who is able to use keen observations and deductive reasoning to solve the most difficult cases. He is also described as eccentric in his habits and serious in his manner, with an arrogant sense of his own abilities. Holmes is sometimes depicted as a world-class expert in forensic chemistry and also as a formidable bareknuckle boxer, sword fighter, and martial arts practitioner.

The enduring popularity of Sherlock Holmes has led to hundreds of adaptations of the stories on stage, screen, radio, and television over the years. Director Guy Ritchie chose to emphasize the character's tough side in his action-packed 2009 film *Sherlock Holmes*. In 2010, the *Sherlock* TV series premiered, starring Benedict Cumberbatch as Sherlock and Martin Freeman as Dr. Watson.

projects. He agreed to star in a comedy called *Due Date*, released in 2010, about an uptight man who must get a ride with an aspiring actor, played by Zach Galifianakis, across the country to be there for the birth of his child. He also agreed to shoot a sequel to *Sherlock Holmes*. *Sherlock Holmes: A Game of Shadows* follows Sherlock and Dr. Watson as they investigate the death of an Austrian prince. The sequel in this franchise also surpassed the earnings of the first movie at the box office.

Avengers Assemble

When Marvel Studios participated in its first comic convention at San Diego Comic-Con, one of the questions that was asked during the panel was if there was potential for characters to cross over to other films—for example, another character appearing in a *Hulk* movie. Feige teased the possibility for an *Avengers* movie, but at that point, it was just a very faint possibility—the first *Iron Man* movie was still two years from being released. Six years after this *Avengers* teaser at San Diego Comic-Con, it was no longer just a possibility and a dream. On May 4, 2012, *The Avengers* was released. From the start, it was an ambitious effort with multiple major superheroes, four of which had their own successful movies by that point (*Iron Man* in 2008 and 2010, *Thor* in 2011, *Captain America: The First Avenger* in 2011, and *The Incredible Hulk* in 2008) sharing the screen.

The Avengers featured Downey in his role as Iron Man, the Hulk (played by Mark Ruffalo), Thor (played by Chris Hemsworth), Captain America (played by Chris Evans), Black Widow (played by Scarlett Johansson), and Hawkeye (played by Jeremy Renner) teaming up against Thor's adopted brother Loki (played by Tom Hiddleston). In the film, Loki steals the Tesseract and opens a portal, which allows an army of the alien race of the Chitauri to invade Earth. The movie received positive reviews, especially for Hiddleston's performance as Loki. Reviewer Peter Bradshaw wrote in the *Guardian* that "Loki steals the film,"[70] while Peter Travers wrote in *Rolling Stone* that "A superhero movie is only as good as its villain, and Hiddleston is dynamite. The role of Loki demands intuition, wit and crazy daring, and Hiddleston brings it. The British actor is a force to reckon with."[71] This movie was what the solo movies such as *Iron Man*, *Thor*, and *Captain America: The First Avenger* were leading up to, and it paid off. While the MCU had released a fair amount of movies before *The Avengers*, this first ensemble film fully proved what the MCU could do and how much of a fan base it had. It earned an impressive $1.5 billion worldwide.

Iron Man 3 was released the year after *The Avengers* and took place immediately following the events in the film. The villain of *Iron Man 3* was the Mandarin, played by Sir Ben Kingsley. However, the treatment of the Mandarin in the movie was something that deeply divided fans, primarily between fans of the comics and fans who did not have much background knowledge of the comics and followed only the MCU. The Mandarin is one of Iron Man's greatest opponents, and some fans were disappointed with the portrayal of him in the movie. Regardless, the movie still made $1.2 billion worldwide, closing out the *Iron Man* trilogy.

Team Cap or Team Iron Man?

After *Iron Man 3*, Downey would not be seen in a MCU movie for two years. In between this time, he starred in *The Judge*, which was released in 2014 and was the first Team Downey film. Downey played Hank Palmer, a lawyer who returns to his hometown because his father has been suspected of murder. However, around this time, Downey also experienced personal heartbreak. Around the time when promotion for the movie was going to kick in, Downey's mother, Elsie, passed away. She was instrumental in helping Downey overcome his addictions, and he posted a tribute to her on social media that reflected on her influence on him throughout the years.

The next year, *Avengers: Age of Ultron* was released. While it did not earn as much as the first movie in the *Avengers* series, it still did incredibly well by making $1.4 billion worldwide. In the film, Tony Stark creates a peacekeeping program called Ultron. However, the program becomes hostile, and the Avengers have to band together in an attempt to defeat the enemy. The story line for *Avengers: Age of Ultron* tied directly into the third movie in the *Captain America* series, called *Captain America: Civil War*, which was released in 2016 with very positive reviews.

In *Avengers: Age of Ultron*, the Battle of Sokovia occurs, with

CHRIS EVANS ROBERT DOWNEY JR. SCARLETT JOHANSSON SEBASTIAN STAN ANTHONY MACKIE DON CHEADLE JEREMY RENNER CHADWICK BOSEMAN PAUL BETTANY ELIZABETH OLSEN AND DANIEL BRÜHL

MARVEL
CAPTAIN AMERICA
CIVIL WAR

DIVIDED WE FALL.
IN 3D, REAL D 3D MAY 6 AND IMAX 3D

Captain America: Civil War featured a prominent role for
Downey, with the focus of the film being the division between
the Avengers who supported Captain America and those who
supported Iron Man. The marketing material, such as this
movie display, also heavily played into the Team Cap or Team
Iron Man debate.

the hostile Ultron program trying to cause global extinction
by raising a portion of the city to the sky and crashing it
down upon Earth. The battle resulted in hundreds of civilian
deaths and was followed by the deaths of dozens of people in
Lagos, Nigeria, in *Captain America: Civil War*. Between these
two battles, the Sokovia Accords were created as an account-
ability system for the Avengers.

Tony Stark supported these accords after the two devastating events that he felt responsible for, while Captain America supported civil liberties. The film details the fallout and splitting of the Avengers between those who were on Captain America's side and those who were on Iron Man's side. The marketing campaigns for the movie also joined fans in the discussion as to which hero's side they were on. The Team Cap or Team Iron Man debate even spread to Downey's and Chris Evans's (Steve Rogers/Captain America) Twitter accounts, with Downey posting humorous Tweets that many fans love him for, such as a picture on April Fool's Day of Iron Man and a phrase next to it saying that he supports Team Cap.

The End of Iron Man

A new addition to the MCU who appeared in *Captain America: Civil War* for the first time was Tom Holland as Peter Parker/Spider-Man. The next year, in 2017, Downey would appear as Spider-Man's mentor in *Spider-Man: Homecoming*. However, with the introduction of new characters such as Spider-Man into the MCU, that also meant that the MCU began closing out the saga of many characters with the end of the initial *Avengers* series. The contracts of many beloved MCU actors, such as Downey, Evans, Hemsworth, and others, were also ending.

Many of these contracts ended with two films—*Avengers: Infinity War*, released in 2018, and *Avengers: Endgame*, released in 2019. Since appearing in *Iron Man* in 2008, Downey has become the face of the MCU and a fan favorite. Additionally, he helped make the MCU what it is today, which has made these last two films in his run as Iron Man both thrilling and saddening for many fans. In these films, Thanos the mad titan is on a mission to acquire all the Infinity Stones (Time, Mind, Power, Soul, Reality, and Space) and use them to wreak destruction on the universe. The cast was massive, with characters from solo movies such as *Black Panther* and *Doctor Strange* joining the Avengers and the Guardians of the Galaxy.

Avengers: Infinity War was massively successful for Downey and the MCU as a whole. The movie broke a

Avengers: Infinity War featured a massive ensemble cast that included the Avengers, the Guardians of the Galaxy, and stars from solo films such as *Doctor Strange*. The movie broke many records.

number of records, including earning $258 million in the first weekend, making it the largest domestic opening for a film at the time of its release. It also earned the honor of being the largest worldwide opening at the time of its release, earning $382 million overseas for a total of $640 million overall for opening weekend.

Looking Forward

With Downey's contract with Marvel ending after *Avengers: Endgame*, he did not waste time adding more movies to his roster. *The Voyage of Doctor Dolittle*, with Downey starring as Dr. John Dolittle, and *Sherlock Holmes 3* are both scheduled for 2020 releases.

Robert Downey Jr. started out at a disadvantage with trying drugs at such a young age and ended up making a series of mistakes in his life. However, he eventually overcame his addictions and turned his life around for good. Downey's struggles throughout these times prove to be an inspiration for people who are also struggling with addiction and feel as though they will not be able to beat it and make something of themselves. While these people may not all become famous actors, Downey is proof that they can get clean, get a good job, and have real family connections. He rose from being an actor whom studios would not cast to being one of the leads in a major movie franchise. Additionally, he became one of the highest-paid actors in Hollywood—a distinction he worked for many years to earn.

Notes

Introduction: Robert Downey Jr.: Box Office Superstar

1. Jim Emerson, "Iron Man," RogerEbert.com, May 2, 2008. www.rogerebert.com/reviews/iron-man.

2. Hilary de Vries, "Channeling Chaplin: It Is the Role of Robert Downey Jr.'s Career—And He Believes the Little Tramp Is With Him," *Los Angeles Times*, December 20, 1992. articles. latimes.com/1992-12-20/entertainment/ca-4268_1_robert-downey-jr.

3. Roger Ebert, "Chaplin," RogerEbert.com, January 8, 1993. www.rogerebert.com/reviews/chaplin-1993.

4. Paul Scott, "From Washed-Up Drug Addict to the $100m Man: How Iron Man Star Robert Downey Jr Turned His Life Around from Prison and Cocaine," DailyMail.com, May 23, 2013. www.dailymail.co.uk/tvshowbiz/article-2330012/How-Iron-Man-star-Robert-Downey-Jr-turned-life-prison-cocaine.html.

5. Quoted in Ben Falk, *Robert Downey Jr.: The Rise and Fall of the Comeback Kid*. London, UK: Portico, 2010, p. 250.

Chapter One: Destined for Films

6. Quoted in Jamie Diamond, "Robert Downey Jr. Is Chaplin (On Screen) and a Child (Off)," *New York Times*, December 20, 1992. www.nytimes.com/1992/12/20/movies/film-robert-downey-jr-is-chaplin-on-screen-and-a-child-off.html.

7. Quoted in Diamond, "Robert Downey Jr. Is Chaplin (On Screen) and a Child (Off)."

8. Quoted in Diamond, "Robert Downey Jr. Is Chaplin (On Screen) and a Child (Off)."

9. Quoted in John Horn, "Robert Downey Jr. Takes One Day at a Time," *Newsweek*, February 11, 2001.

www.newsweek.com/robert-downey-jr-takes-one-day-time-155277.

10. Quoted in Kyle Smith, "Hitting Bottom: Robert Downey Jr. Makes Prison the Latest Stop in a Life of Misspent Promise," *People*, February 14, 2000. people.com/archive/hitting-bottom-vol-53-no-6/.

11. Quoted in Falk, *Robert Downey Jr.*, p. 23.

12. Quoted in Diamond, "Robert Downey Jr. Is Chaplin (On Screen) and a Child (Off)."

13. Quoted in Joan Juliet Buck, "An Exceptional Talent: After Dark Years of Addiction, Rehab, and Prison, Robert Downey Jr.," *Vogue*, April 2006, p. 370.

14. Quoted in Scott Raab, "Robert Downey Jr.: The Second Greatest Actor in the World," *Esquire*, November 10, 2009. www.esquire.com/news-politics/a6651/robert-downey-jr-interview-1209/.

15. Quoted in *Rolling Stone*, "Dropout Boogie: 14 Celebs Who Never Got Their Degree," *Rolling Stone*, May 28, 2014. www.rollingstone.com/culture/culture-lists/dropout-boogie-14-celebs-who-never-got-their-degree-14864/robert-downey-jr-3-207790/.

16. Quoted in Buck, "An Exceptional Talent," p. 370.

Chapter Two: A Rising Star

17. Quoted in Lowri Williams, "Sarah Jessica Parker Knows All About Addiction ... Thanks to Robert Downey Jr.," *EntertainmentWise*, March 16, 2006. www.entertainmentwise.com/news/14640/sarah-jessica-parker-knows-all.

18. David Denby, "More than Zero," *New York*, November 23, 1987, p. 104.

19. Quoted in Diamond, "Robert Downey Jr. Is Chaplin (On Screen) and a Child (Off)."

20. Quoted in Jon Wilde, "More than Skin Deep," *Guardian*, November 8, 2003. www.guardian.co.uk/film/2003/nov/08/features.

21. Quoted in Bernard Weintraub, "Sarah Jessica Parker on Stardom, Dating, and the Baby She'd Love to Have," *Redbook*, July 1, 1996, p. 54.

22. Quoted in Buck, "An Exceptional Talent," p. 370.

23. Quoted in Falk, *Robert Downey Jr.*, p. 72.

24. Vincent Canby, "Robert Downey Jr. in Charlie Chaplin Life Story," *New York Times*, December 25, 1992. movies.nytimes.com/movie/review?res=9E0CE5D7153CF936A15751C1A964958260.

25. Jeffrey M. Anderson, "Resurrecting the Tramp," Combustible Celluloid, accessed on September 6, 2018. www.combustiblecelluloid.com/archive/chaplin92.shtml.

26. Quoted in Rebecca Winters Keegan, "Why Is This Man Smiling?," *TIME*, April 28, 2008, p. 77.

27. Quoted in Keegan, "Why Is This Man Smiling?," p. 77.

28. Quoted in Buck, "An Exceptional Talent," p. 370.

Chapter Three: The Road to Recovery

29. Stephen Holden, "The Last Party: About America as a Family That's Dysfunctional," *New York Times*, August 27, 1993. movies.nytimes.com/movie/review?res=9F0CEED61439F934A1575BC0A965958260.

30. Todd McCarthy, "Short Cuts," *Variety*, September 7, 1993. www.variety.com/index.asp?layout=review&reviewid=VE1117901214&categoryid=31&query=short+cuts&display=short+cuts&cs=1.

31. Janet Maslin, "A Yuppie Haunted (Really) by Other People's Problems," *New York Times*, August 13, 1993. movies.nytimes.com/movie/review?_r=2&res=9F0CE1DF1F38F930A2575BC0A965958260&partner=Rotten%20Tomatoes.

32. Jack Mathews, "'Hugo Pool' Doesn't Reflect Well on Downeys Jr. and Sr.," *Los Angeles Times*, December 12, 1997. articles. latimes.com/1997/dec/12/entertainment/ca-63148.

33. Janet Maslin, "Two Girls and a Guy: The Love Triangle as One-Man Show," *New York Times*, April 24, 1998. movies. nytimes.com/movie/review?res=9F07E2DF103FF937A157 57C0A96E958260.

34. Quoted in David Hochman, "Downey and Out in Beverly Hills," *Entertainment Weekly*, March 27, 1998, p. 34.

35. Quoted in Hochman, "Downey and Out in Beverly Hills," p. 34.

36. Quoted in Hochman, "Downey and Out in Beverly Hills," p. 34.

37. Quoted in Jeffrey Ressner, "From Hollywood to Hell and Back," *TIME*, April 27, 1998, p. 66.

38. Quoted in Ressner, "From Hollywood to Hell and Back," p. 66.

39. Quoted in Ressner, "From Hollywood to Hell and Back," p. 66.

40. Quoted in Falk, *Robert Downey Jr.*, p. 165.

41. Quoted in Wilde, "More than Skin Deep."

42. Quoted in Andrew Gumbel, "Downey Jr. May Never Act Again Following Dismissal from 'Ally McBeal,'" *Independent*, April 26, 2001. www.independent.co.uk/news/world/americas/downey-jr-may-never-act-again-after-dismissal-from-ally-mcbeal-682655.html.

43. "About Prop 36," California Proposition 36, accessed on August 14, 2018. www.uclaisap.org/prop36/html/about-prop-36.html.

Chapter Four: Making a Comeback

44. Quoted in Buck, "An Exceptional Talent," p. 370.

45. Quoted in Sarah Kurchak, "How Wing Chun Helped Robert Downey Jr. Battle Addiction," Vice, February 8, 2016.

fightland.vice.com/blog/how-wing-chun-helped-robert-downey-jr-battle-addiction.

46. Quoted in Kevin West, "Mr. Clean: Married, Sober, and on the Road to Salvation, Robert Downey Jr. Pulls No Punches," *W*, March 2007, p. 392.

47. Quoted in Tricia Johnson, "Robert Downey Jr. Faces Life After Prison," *Entertainment Weekly*, August 9, 2000. ew.com/article/2000/08/09/robert-downey-jr-faces-life-after-prison/.

48. Quoted in Jason Lynch, "Back from the Edge," *People*, November 10, 2003. people.com/archive/back-from-the-edge-vol-60-no-19/.

49. Quoted in Lynch, "Back from the Edge."

50. Quoted in West, "Mr. Clean," p. 392.

51. Quoted in Natasha Stoynoff, "The Comeback Kid," *People*, May 19, 2008. people.com/archive/the-comeback-kid-vol-69-no-19/.

52. Quoted in Hilary DeVries, "Robert Downey Jr.: The Album," *New York Times*, November 21, 2004. www.nytimes.com/2004/11/21/arts/music/21devr.html?pagewanted=1&_r=1&oref=slogin&adxnnlx=1210518255-AHT6ACtNjm%20MebN5u6Ef8g.

53. Manohla Dargis, "Hunting a Killer as the Age of Aquarius Dies," *New York Times*, March 2, 2007. www.nytimes.com/2007/03/02/movies/02zodi.html?mtrref=www.google.com.

54. Benjamin Svetkey, "Entertainer of the Year: Robert Downey Jr.," *Entertainment Weekly*, November 21, 2008. ew.com/article/2008/11/14/robert-downey-jr-entertainer-year/.

Chapter Five: "I Am Iron Man"

55. Quoted in Svetkey, "Entertainer of the Year: Robert Downey Jr."

56. Don Kaye, "The Definitive Timeline of Bringing Iron Man to the Screen 10 Years Ago," May 2, 2018. www.syfy.com/syfywire/the-definitive-timeline-of-bringing-iron-man-to-the-screen-10-years-ago.

57. Quoted in Rachel Abramowitz, "Robert Downey Jr. Is Ready to Play the Hero in 'Iron Man,'" *Los Angeles Times*, April 27, 2008. www.latimes.com/entertainment/la-ca-downey27apr27-story.html.

58. Abramowitz, "Robert Downey Jr. Is Ready to Play the Hero in 'Iron Man.'"

59. Quoted in Rich Cohen, "The Ride of His Life," *Vanity Fair*, October 2014. www.vanityfair.com/hollywood/2014/09/robert-downey-jr-addiction-children.

60. Quoted in Keegan, "Why Is This Man Smiling?," p. 77.

61. Quoted in Scott Raab, "The Quiet One: May God Bless and Keep Robert Downey Jr. and, If You're Up There, We're Not Kidding This Time," *Esquire*, March 2007, p. 149.

62. Quoted in Keegan, "Why Is This Man Smiling?," p. 77.

63. Quoted in Zack Sharf, "Robert Downey Jr. Improvised the Original 'Iron Man' Twist Ending, and Kevin Feige Says It Changed the MCU Forever," IndieWire, July 20, 2018. www.indiewire.com/2018/07/kevin-feige-robert-downey-jr-improvised-iron-man-twist-ending-1201986093/.

64. Sharf, "Robert Downey Jr. Improvised the Original 'Iron Man' Twist Ending, and Kevin Feige Says It Changed the MCU Forever."

65. Quoted in Stoynoff, "The Comeback Kid."

66. Quoted in Svetkey, "Entertainer of the Year."

67. Manohla Dargis, "*The Soloist*: Struggle and Rescue, a Duet in Sharps and Minors," *New York Times*, April 23, 2009. movies.nytimes.com/2009/04/24/movies/24solo.html.

68. Quoted in Falk, *Robert Downey Jr.*, p. 237.

69. Quoted in Josh Rottenberg, "Extreme Holmes Makeover," *Entertainment Weekly*, November 20, 2009. ew.com/article/2009/11/20/sherlock-holmes-gets-action-movie-treatment/.

70. Peter Bradshaw, "The Avengers—Review," *Guardian*, May 3, 2012. www.theguardian.com/film/2012/apr/26/avengers-assemble-review.

71. Peter Travers, "The Avengers," *Rolling Stone*, April 30, 2012. www.rollingstone.com/movies/movie-reviews/the-avengers-118986/.

Robert Downey Jr. Year by Year

1965

Robert Downey Jr. is born on April 4.

1970

Downey appears in a small role as a puppy in the movie *Pound*.

1983

Downey plays Stewart in *Baby It's You*.

1984

Downey plays Lee in *Firstborn* and starts dating actress Sarah Jessica Parker.

1985

Downey picks up a significant role as Ian in *Weird Science*, begins a friendship with actor Anthony Michael Hall, and becomes a *Saturday Night Live* cast member for one season.

1986

Downey plays a prominent role as Derek in *Back to School*.

1987

Downey stars in his first leading role as Jack Jericho in *The Pick-Up Artist*.

1990

Downey stars in *Air America* with Mel Gibson.

1991

Sarah Jessica Parker ends their seven-year relationship.

1992

Downey stars in and receives praise for his role as Charlie Chaplin in *Chaplin* and meets and marries Deborah Falconer.

1993

Downey is nominated for an Academy Award for Best Actor in a Leading Role for his work in *Chaplin* and takes on roles in *Short Cuts*, *Heart and Souls*, and *The Last Party*; his son Indio is born in September.

1995

Downey appears in *Home for the Holidays* and stars as Robert Merivel in *Restoration*.

1996

Deborah Falconer leaves Downey; Downey is arrested and ordered to receive treatment at Exodus Recovery Center, and he hosts *Saturday Night Live*.

1997

Downey stars in *Hugo Pool*, is released from the rehabilitation facility, stars in *Two Girls and a Guy*, suffers a relapse, and is sentenced to prison.

1998

Downey is released from jail in March, goes from jail to a live-in rehabilitation center, and is released from the rehabilitation facility in August; *The Gingerbread Man* and *U.S. Marshals* are released.

1999

Downey relapses into drug use and is sentenced to the California Substance Abuse Treatment Facility and State Prison.

2000

Downey joins the cast of *Ally McBeal*; he is arrested in November.

2001

Downey wins a Golden Globe for Best Performance by an Actor in a Supporting Role in a Series, Mini-Series or Motion Picture Made for Television; is arrested in April and then fired from *Ally McBeal*; and is sentenced to one year at Wavelengths International rehabilitation facility and three years of probation.

2002

Downey completes yearlong program at Wavelengths.

2003

The Singing Detective is released; Downey meets Susan Levin on the set of *Gothika*.

2004

Downey's album, *The Futurist*, is released.

2005

Downey and Levin are married on August 27; *Good Night, and Good Luck* is released; and Downey stars in *Kiss Kiss Bang Bang*.

2006

Downey stars as Dr. Kozak in Disney's *The Shaggy Dog*.

2007

Downey stars in *Charlie Bartlett* and plays journalist Paul Avery in *Zodiac*.

2008

Iron Man is released, earning more than $585 million worldwide, and Downey is catapulted into superstardom; he also stars in *Tropic Thunder*.

2009

Downey is nominated for his second Academy Award for Best Actor in a Supporting Role for *Tropic Thunder*; he also stars in *The Soloist* and *Sherlock Holmes*.

2010

Downey wins a Golden Globe Award for Best Performance by an Actor in a Motion Picture—Musical or Comedy for his performance in *Sherlock Holmes*; *Iron Man 2* is released; and *Due Date* is released.

2012

Downey's son Exton Elias is born; *The Avengers* is released and becomes one of the highest-grossing films of all time.

2014

Downey's daughter Avri Roel is born; Downey stars in *The Judge*, a Team Downey film, and his mother, Elsie, passes away.

2015

Avengers: Age of Ultron is released.

2016

Captain America: Civil War is released, the marketing campaign of which encourages fans to choose Team Cap or Team Iron Man.

2017

Spider-Man: Homecoming is released.

2018

Avengers: Infinity War is released, breaking records and adding another MCU movie to the list of the highest-grossing films of all time.

2019

Avengers: Endgame is released, ending many MCU actors' franchise contracts.

For More Information

Books

Falk, Ben. *Robert Downey Jr.: The Rise and Fall of the Comeback Kid.* London, UK: Portico, 2010.
This unauthorized biography examines Downey's formative experiences and their impact on his life and career.

Howe, Sean. *Marvel Comics: The Untold Story.* New York, NY: Harper Perennial, 2012.
A must-have book for Marvel fans, this book details the history of Marvel from the early days of Timely Comics to recent years with the MCU.

Thomas, John Rhett. *The Art of Iron Man.* London, UK: Titan Books, 2018.
This official companion to Downey's *Iron Man* series offers an exclusive behind the scenes look at the making of the film. Thomas's book includes exclusive photos and interviews with essential people who worked on the films, including Jon Favreau, special effects workers, designers, artists, and more.

Watson, Stephanie. *Robert Downey Jr.: Blockbuster Movie Star.* Minneapolis, MN: ABDO Publishing Company, 2012.
Watson's book examines Downey's life and acting career.

Websites

Marvel University
(www.marvel.com/watch/digital-series/marvel-university)
Many of Marvel's characters and stories, especially Tony Stark/
Iron Man, were inspired by science and technology in the real
world. This official Marvel video series talks with experts to
explore the technology and science behind these stories so
readers and viewers can gain a deeper appreciation for their
favorite characters and story lines.

Robert Downey Jr. on Instagram
(www.instagram.com/robertdowneyjr/?hl=en)
Downey's official Instagram page has behind the scenes photos
on his movie sets and personal photos.

Robert Downey Jr. on the Internet Movie Database
(www.imdb.com/name/nm0000375/)
This valuable resource for fans of Downey's work shows every
movie he has made an appearance in and what movies are
upcoming, as well as a brief biography and trivia on the actor.

Robert Downey Jr. on Twitter
(twitter.com/RobertDowneyJr)
Downey's official Twitter page has updates on movies he is working on, information about charities he is working with, and
humorous posts that keep fans amused.

Index

Picture Credits

Cover Jon Kopaloff/Film Magic/Getty Images; p. 8 Frazer Harrison/ Getty Images; p. 10 Rich Polk/Getty Images for Disney; p. 13 Jimi Celeste/Patrick McMullan via Getty Images; p. 14 Ron Galella, Ltd./WireImage/Getty Images; p. 17 Tommaso Boddi/Getty Images for Disney; p. 21 Barry King/WireImage/Getty Images; p. 23 20th Century-Fox/Getty Images; p. 26 Sunset Boulevard/ Getty Images; p. 28 Carolco Pictures/Getty Images; p. 31 Movie Poster Image Art/Getty Images; p. 33 Barry King/Liaison/Getty Images; p. 36 Frank Trapper/Corbis via Getty Images; p. 37 Fotos International/Getty Images; p. 39 Getty Images/Handout/ Hulton Archive/Getty Images; p. 42 Dave Allocca/DMI/The LIFE Picture Collection/Getty Images; pp. 48, 58 Featureflash Photo Agency/Shutterstock.com; p. 53 Paul Harris/Getty Images; p. 56 George Pimentel/WireImage/Getty Images; p. 61 Everett Collection/Shutterstock.com; p. 62 Kevin Winter/Getty Images; p. 63 M. Caulfield/WireImage/Getty Images; p. 67 Charley Gallay/Getty Images for Disney; p. 68 Steve Mack/FilmMagic/ Getty Images; p. 71 Albert L. Ortega/Getty Images; p. 73 Kathy Hutchins/Shutterstock.com; p. 78 Jon Furniss/WireImage/Getty Images; p. 82 Gabe Ginsberg/WireImage/Getty Images; p. 84 tanpanamanoob/Shutterstock.com.

About the Author

Nicole Horning is a huge Marvel fan who was on the side of Team Cap. In between reading Marvel comics, watching movies in the MCU, and attending comic conventions, she writes books for young adults. She holds a bachelor's degree in English and a master's degree in special education from D'Youville College in Buffalo, New York. She lives in Western New York with her cats Khaleesi and Evie and writes fiction in the rest of her free time.